FIREPLACE SECRETS

FIREPLACE SECRETS

A Problem-Solving Manual for Fireplaces and Chimneys

MARK SWANN

Copyright © 2016 by Mark Swann.

Library of Congress Control Number: 2015920249
ISBN: Hardcover   978-1-5144-3241-9
               Softcover   978-1-5144-3240-2
               eBook   978-1-5144-3239-6

Print information available on the last page.

Rev. date: 12/29/2015

To order additional copies of this book, contact:
Xlibris
1-888-795-4274
www.Xlibris.com
Orders@Xlibris.com
731442

For Diane

CONTENTS

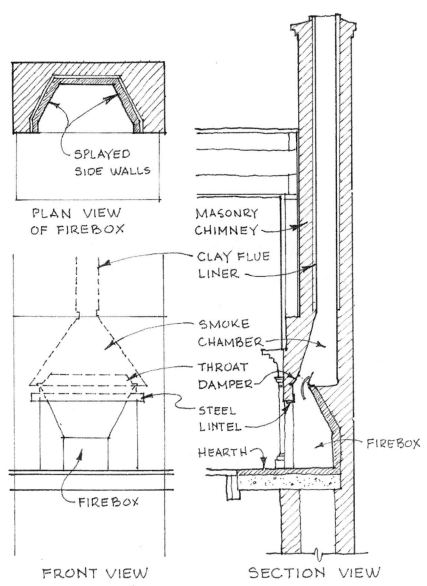

SPLAYED
SIDE WALLS

PLAN VIEW
OF FIREBOX

MASONRY
CHIMNEY

CLAY FLUE
LINER

SMOKE
CHAMBER

THROAT
DAMPER

STEEL
LINTEL

HEARTH

FIREBOX

FIREBOX

FRONT VIEW

SECTION VIEW

TYPICAL MASONRY FIREPLACE CHIMNEY SYSTEM

FIGURE 1

A fireplace/chimney system has two parts: the firebox where burning takes place and a duct or channel for removing smoke and gasses, the chimney flue. The two are not the same size. The firebox opening is usually ten times as large as the chimney flue. This is known as the fireplace to chimney ratio.

The genius of a fireplace is that it can burn inside your house without smoking. It can do this because it has three points of transition where smoke and gasses are funneled into ever-smaller spaces. They are in the firebox, (1) where the angled sidewalls form a funnel leading to the back wall and into the throat; (2) where the throat damper forms a funnel leading into the damper opening; and (3) where the smoke chamber funnels into the flue liner. Without this funneling, the chimney would have to be as large as the fireplace opening, the design of some early fireplace/chimney systems. See opening of Chapter V.

INTRODUCTION

This book is a fireplace/chimney manual. It will describe the different parts, their function and malfunction. It will suggest various ways to correct problems.

This book is intended for anyone with a fireplace, for chimney sweeps, for architects who design fireplaces, for builders who oversee new fireplace construction, and for fireplace builders themselves. This is not a coffee table book. It is not about how fireplaces and chimneys look. It's about how and why they work and why they often don't.

As you will see, building a new fireplace correctly is a science. But correcting a flawed fireplace enough so it works acceptably is an art.

My qualifications to write such a book are my thirty years as a chimney sweep and fireplace doctor and builder in Washington, DC. One customer called me "the fireplace whisperer." During this time I made important discoveries about fireplaces, which have never been described before: first, about the best ways to solve smoke problems and, second, how to make fireplaces into real heaters. My focus is on masonry/brick fireplaces, not the cheaper, less versatile, less interesting factory-made fireplace, the prefab.

About a third of fireplaces smoke, some badly, but most only moderately, some all the time, some occasionally. And, though a smoking problem may seem random, there are always explanations and solutions, despite what some contractors say that some fireplaces can never be made to work. The information in this book disproves this idea.

I find it useful to think of fireplace systems as machines even though each one is constructed individually. Luckily, this means that any brick fireplace, unlike the prefab fireplace, can also be modified, if necessary, on site, at reasonable cost. This book describes the best ways to do this.

As you will see, most of the discoveries I have made simply could not have been made by just thinking about fireplace problems. The mysteries of fireplaces were certainly not revealed to me by my reading of scores of books on the subject. It was necessary to be personally engaged in that demanding, frustrating, often nasty, brutal environment of fireplaces and chimneys. If I'd just hired people and tried to train them to do the right thing, I doubt that I would have ever learned anything useful. It would have been the blind leading the blind. The unknowns were too numerous.

It helps to keep in mind that it is exactly what we love about the fireplace—that it is an *open fire* burning inside our houses—that creates the challenge. A potbellied or airtight stove almost never smokes and is more heat efficient. But no one wants to gather 'round a stove to sing carols and party, to celebrate. Or even meditate... We want the primal, open fireplace experience—the dancing, popping, crackling flames, the blazing heat, the crazy colors, the low register hum. I guess our love of the open fire just means we are all romantics (or cavemen!) at heart.

And, although I had nary a college course on fireplaces or their construction, I believe my college education proved useful in tracking down the evolution and history of fireplaces and putting my discoveries in context. I also want to mention it because so many customers appreciated that this self-described "chimney guy" working on their fireplaces, down and dirty and black as coal, was a Harvard and Cambridge man. Word of mouth always carries the day.

CHAPTER I

SMOKING FIXES FOR HOMEOWNERS

CONTENTS

Chimneys perform differently when hot. Heat makes them "draw," the greater the heat the harder the draw, thus merely increasing chimney temperatures can stop a fireplace from smoking.

GLASS DOORS

But how best to increase chimney temperatures? The quickest, most obvious way is with glass doors! First, a regular fire is laid. It is lit, and then, immediately, the doors are closed, leaving the vents at the bottom of the door's frame open to supply air and oxygen. The goal is to heat up the chimney until it starts to draw. Sometimes, especially if there is lots of cold air coming down the chimney, wisps of smoke will leak out around the doors for a few seconds. But, usually, in less than half a minute, the chimney will start drawing strongly, in fact very like a blast furnace because the air is being pulled into the bottom of the fireplace and through the burning fuel. At that point the doors should be opened. The fire will then slow down but, almost always, the now warmed chimney will keep drawing hard enough so that no smoke at all will leak out of the fireplace. See Figure 2.

DOORS OPEN, FIRE LAID, FIRE LIT
FIREPLACE IS SMOKING.

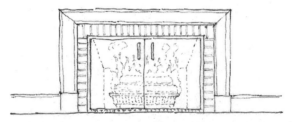

DOORS CLOSED WITH AIR VENTS AT BOTTOM OPEN
SMOKE AT FIRST SWIRLING AROUND BEHIND DOORS

WHEN CHIMNEY STARTS TO DRAW
USUALLY IN LESS THAN A MINUTE
OPEN DOORS

CORRECT USE OF GLASS DOORS

FIGURE 2

For some mysterious reason, this is one of the best kept secrets in the world of fireplaces. Maybe it's secret because it must be done in a certain way as the following cautionary tale reveals.

GLASS DOORS A DOUBLE-EDGED SWORD

I once looked at a fireplace that had hardly been used although built some 40 years before. This is almost always an indication of a serious smoking problem. The new owner of the house wanted to know if he could start using it. (Most people assume a fireplace will work just because it's there. I suspect he had tried and got lots of smoke.) Well, I checked it out at the fireplace and at the chimney top. The fireplace itself was adequate. The chimney was also an adequate 30' tall—tall chimneys draw harder—but with the smallest flue liner. The bigger problem was the inside of the chimney. The sloppy chimney builders had failed to clean off the excess mortar that had squeezed out of the joints between the flue liners. The result was that the flue area was significantly reduced. See Figure 3.

We can say with certainty that this fireplace should never work without smoking. But if the excess mortar could be knocked off—not easily done but possible—and then glass doors installed and employed *at the beginning of the fire* to heat up the chimney, there was a very good chance it could be made to work without smoking. My recommendation to the homeowner was to, first, fix the chimney and, second, install doors. As I was leaving, the man's wife returned. He was so smart he was able to explain to her in his own words exactly what I had just explained to him, including all the reasoning and the math, a grasp of the issues that had taken me a couple of decades to master.

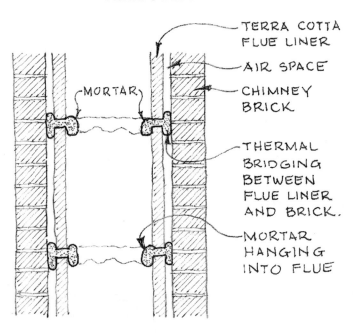

TERRA COTTA FLUE LINER

AIR SPACE

MORTAR

CHIMNEY BRICK

THERMAL BRIDGING BETWEEN FLUE LINER AND BRICK.

MORTAR HANGING INTO FLUE

FAULTY FLUE LINER INSTALLATION

FIGURE 3

Although most of what he told her seemed to go over her head—and his enthusiasm seemed to make her anxious—I was impressed that he had remembered everything so well. Surely this was one of the smartest customers I had ever had, I thought, an amazing quick study.

What happened next was not good, not impressive, not exactly smart. (His wife's anxiety was, well..., well-founded.) I had assumed I would be involved at each step of the job so I guess

I must have failed to impress on him strongly enough that the repairs to the chimney were the absolutely necessary first step.

Disregarding my advice and without informing me what he planned to do, he bought and installed doors and then tried to use the fireplace. It actually worked but whenever he opened the doors, it would smoke badly. So he just kept the doors closed except when adding more logs. The chimney eventually got so hot it lit his house on fire.

Running a fireplace with the doors closed heats the entire fireplace/chimney system, including sections that are not designed for lots of heat. During normal operation, most of a fireplace's radiant heat, for example, is projected into the house. With the glass doors closed only around 40% gets through the glass; the rest remains within the system. Worse still, hardly any house air, which is at much lower temperature than smoke and combustion gasses, is drawn into the fireplace and chimney.

A little knowledge is a dangerous thing.

I have described how the inside of the chimney was severely constricted because the excess mortar had not been trimmed off. But there was also excess mortar on the outside of the flue liner, which meant that, instead of the usual modest insulating air space of around 1/2" between the outside of the liner and the brick of the chimney, there was a significant conductive pathway at every joint for heat to travel from inside the flue liner to outside the flue liner to the brick and, it turned out, through these brick to nearby wood.

When I've tried to look at this unfortunate incident objectively, I'm annoyed with myself that, if our roles had been reversed, I might well have done exactly the same thing as this man, assuming that I'd had no experience with these things and, of course, I too would have set my house on fire.

That heat could change the performance of a fireplace system so radically is an almost irresistible idea. Yet it is hardly known to the public in more than a general way. Its significance is not even known by most fireplace stores selling glass doors. Imagine not knowing how your most powerful product works!

Now setting your house on fire the way I've described here is hard to do. I'm pretty sure this man—I call him "my cowboy"— kept the fireplace going for at least 3 hours. He must have been thoroughly delighted with himself until...

The only good thing about most fireplace/chimney fires—they are usually very small and hardly ever dangerous, as I will show in Chapter VI—is that the fireplace operator is almost always right there on the scene and in full attendance, stoking and enjoying the fire. No one was killed or hurt in this fire and only modest property damage occurred. The firemen arrived promptly. Insurance paid for all of the damage, an indication to me that accidents of this kind are rare. In fact, using your fireplace is remarkably safe, even if you do something stupid, probably safer than driving a couple of miles up the road to buy a gallon of milk. There are fewer variables not under your control.

But it helps to have a basic understanding of the technology, a job this book should fulfill.

Despite the potential for misuse, glass doors are the single most effective piece of equipment for solving fireplace smoking. They are not cheap, however, ranging in price from $350 to more than $1,000, depending on the quality and size. On the other hand, they are widely available and relatively easy to install using the hardware furnished by the door manufacturers. They are the consummate quick fix.

THE EXTREME EVENT

In my view, lighting your house on fire as "my cowboy" did is what I call an "extreme event"—very, very rare but very illustrative of some basic fireplace/chimney truths. Had this chimney been in compliance with that part of the building code, which requires a 2"air space between the outside of the chimney and any combustible, this extreme event could not have occurred, even though the interior of the chimney was built incorrectly and the glass doors were utilized in a very foolish way. But many chimneys do have wood nearby or even pressed right against their outsides, which, under extraordinary circumstances, can catch fire. I consider the odds of this happening very low.

I have encountered other homeowners who were running their fireplaces with closed doors to no bad effect. I hope they stopped the bad habit after I'd explained the risk, however remote.

Besides being a useful tool to overcome smoking, there are other benefits to glass doors. Most of them also have mesh screens or screen doors in addition to the glass doors, which is a reminder to be vigilant about flying sparks when you're not in full attendance. If not contained inside the fireplace, these can launch themselves out of the firebox and beyond the outer hearth and actually set your house on fire or, at a minimum, singe your rugs or pockmark your wood floor. A second benefit is that you can shut the doors at the end of a fire—when you only have hot coals—which will prevent the hot chimney from needlessly drawing tons of warmed air out of your house all night which in turn pulls cold outside air to displace the air lost up the chimney. Without glass doors (or some other means—see Chapter V) this scenario cools the whole house and only stops when we close the damper the next morning. A third reason to have glass doors is if you have a cat. Many cats find the ashes in a fireplace irresistible. Some will use it as kitty litter and others for an ash bath. Ashes can end up spread all over the house, some of it as cute, little footprints. It's crucial to have a foolproof way to keep your cats out of your fireplace.

BUYING GLASS DOORS
The first step is to measure the fireplace opening. Glass doors typically overlap the opening about an inch or slightly more on each side and 1/2 inch to an inch on the top. There are standard sizes. These will be much less expensive than custom-made sizes. Glass door stores need exact measurements of your fireplace opening. There are many different styles and manufacturers.

Doors work best if the surface—the fireplace surround—they are set against is smooth, not rough or irregular. For example, if the fireplace surround is uneven stone, the doors will not naturally make an airtight seal. Doors come with strips of insulation, which can, if needed, be inserted between the frame of the doors and the surround. While it's preferable that the doors be fairly airtight when closed, they will still more or less work in overcoming a smoke problem even if they are not.

If a standard size doors are not quite tall enough for your fireplace, a one-inch riser bar can be used to elevate them. Again, this is much cheaper than buying custom-sized doors.
For a method of installing doors in the best possible way, see Chapter XI.

In addition to my warning about using the fireplace doors in the closed position for more than 2-3 minutes, I have another warning. Even though they are made of tempered glass, sudden increases in temperature can make their glass shatter. This typically happens only at the end of a fire. So, do it gradually, that is, half close them for 5 minutes before closing them all the way. It's advisable never to close them at all if there are still flames higher than ½".

In times past, all doors had air vents on the bottom of the frame. Today, some doors have no air vents. I recommend doors with air vents whether or not you're using the doors to heat the chimney.

Before rushing out and buying glass doors, however, read on to determine how severe your smoking problem actually is and what might be your other options. (Doors are not everyone's first choice for fixing a smoking problem, mainly because they change the look of the fireplace. They are not my first choice for that reason. Some people, however, like the look of doors.)

Smoking occurs on a continuum, i.e., some smoking is so slight that it stops within a few seconds as the chimney heats up, which points to other measures short of doors. Other smoking is so gross and relentless that doors become one of the best choices not requiring fireplace reconstruction.

WHY CHIMNEYS WORK

The reason a chimney draws all the time, even with no fire in the fireplace, is that there is slightly more air pressure at the fireplace than at the chimney top, 20 to 30 feet higher. We have gravity to thank for this, air being denser near the surface of the Earth and lighter as we gain altitude. The air pressure difference is very modest but enough to make the system work if everything else has been designed and constructed correctly. When we add heat, however, we, in effect, supercharge the drawing power. See Figure 4.

I had commissioned this graph on order to demonstrate the relationship of heat to velocity. What floored me was just how much small increases in heat affected velocity. I had imagined something like a 30-degree angle on the plotted graph to start with and then starting to flatten from there. Well, the first 80 degrees F. were not even a 70-degree angle. The next 80 degrees F were 45 degrees. And the next 80 degrees F. finally flattened enough to be considered an angle of 30 degrees. (These are all rough measurements of the plotted line.) From the steepness of the plotted line up to 200 degrees F, you can see just how dramatically even a little added heat improves chimney performance.

Clearly, almost immediately, the full size of the chimney flue was not required to prevent the fireplace from smoking. And the amount of flue needed to handle all the smoke kept decreasing as the temperature of the gases increased.

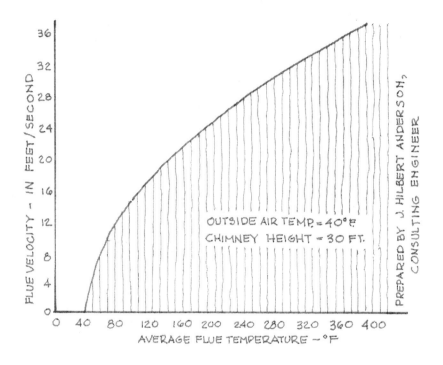

RELATIONSHIP BETWEEN
CHIMNEY TEMPERATURE AND
SMOKE / GAS VELOCITY

FIGURE 4

THE SMOKE PLATE OR SMOKE GUARD

While using glass doors the way I've described is not common knowledge, another fix, the use of a smoke plate (or smoke guard) is well known.

A smoke plate decreases the size of the fireplace opening, which makes the chimney draw harder because of the improved fireplace/chimney ratio and can thus overcome the smoking. (I mention these ratios again in Chapter III, V and IX.) While any reduction in fireplace opening size makes a difference, reducing the height of the fireplace opening is the most effective because usually the smoke is leaking out only across the top of the fireplace. I call this kind of smoking "structural" because it's caused by design and/or construction flaws in the fireplace. See Figure 5.

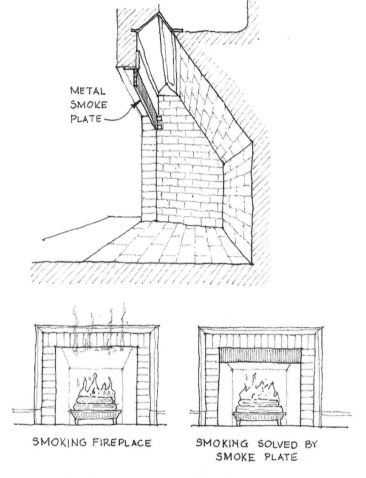

METAL SMOKE PLATE

SMOKING FIREPLACE   SMOKING SOLVED BY SMOKE PLATE

SMOKING FIREPLACE SOLVED BY SMOKE PLATE

FIGURE 5

The particular smoke plate I have in mind is 4" tall, factory-made, and available at many hardware stores, most fireplace shops, and on line. Installation, which involves adjusting the plate's length with a spring, is straightforward. It can solve nearly a quarter of smoke problems. And it should only cost around $50. This is a real bargain.

If the 4" smoke plate *almost completely* solved the smoke problem, I would go buy what I call a tall (also 4"), true grate. See Figure 6.

HOT COALS
FALL THROUGH

FALSE GRATE

HOT COALS

TRUE GRATE

GRATES

FIGURE 6

Notice how the cross members of the *true* grate are much closer together than those of the false grate. From a technical point of view, a true grate leads to more complete combustion because the unburned wood sits right on top of the hottest embers. With a *false* grate, most of the embers drop down to the hearth, away from the unburned wood.

A clean burn delivers more heat and less smoke, both very desirable. A fireplace that's smoking just a little can often be fixed by *the height* of a tall, true grate and the cleaner burn it makes possible. Even if it doesn't solve the smoking completely, it always gives you improvement.

It's a little counterintuitive that just elevating a fire could help with smoking. But it does, I believe, because it's as if you had made the firebox somewhat less tall.

Before you buy a grate, measure the inside of your fireplace. Make sure the narrow side of the grate fits snugly against the back wall. The next consideration is the depth of the grate. You definitely don't want it to stick out beyond the front of the fireplace! There are two standard grate depths, 12" and 16". Unless the fireplace is quite deep—18" or more—I tend to pick a 12" grate. One of the strategies for solving smoke problems is to keep most of the fire itself as near the back wall as possible, which the 12" grate always does better than the 16" grate. The flaw with the 12" grate is that the charge of wood you can burn at any one time is smaller. As a general rule, the grate is most important to prevent smoking at the beginning of a fire before the chimney has heated up and is drawing hard.

LIGHTING THAT FIRE

In many ways, lighting that first fire in a fireplace new to you is like your first step in love. Will the chimney draw? Or will you end up with a smoky mess? The fireplace may look charming and beautiful, but that doesn't mean you are going to transition into blazing harmony. The uncertainty and suspense with any new fireplace can be huge.

As I've explained, fireplace smoking falls on a continuum. The important principle to keep in mind is that the solution for most smoking problems involves heating up the chimney. The worst smoking cases simply cannot be managed without what I consider extreme measures like glass doors. The less challenging just need a little coaxing—a way to get a little heat going up the flue—to warm things up and get things started. I did some work for a man in Philadelphia who kept an antique blowtorch near at hand for this purpose. A lady in DC always uses her hair dryer. As they say, whatever works for you and your fireplace... However, the more conventional approach is to simply hold one or more newspaper torches up through the damper.

If you have used a fireplace before, chances are it will behave just as it always did. If it started quickly without any smoke, it's very likely it will start the same way again. If it was a slow, smoky starter before, it most likely will still be a slow, smoky starter. Fireplaces are like people: they don't change much. The only caution with a familiar fireplace is to be sure the damper is open, that you remember and honor her particular peculiarities, and if you've not worked her for a year or more, to be sure no one has built a nest in her chimney.

The true challenge comes with any fireplace that is new to you. You need to figure out what works. Or, if it works at all and, as you begin, it is important to be prepared for the worst. I strongly suggest that you begin any new fireplace relationship with a small test fire—just a few handfuls of twigs.

As you approach things know that house air will either be moving up the chimney, or outside air coming down the chimney, or, thirdly, the chimney may be in that rare, neutral zone where there is no movement either way. The place to begin is with the newspaper torch held up through the damper, up the flu. If that smoke is drawn up the chimney, great. Then, for good measure, crack a window or door. Finally light your small test fire and then monitor for smoke along the top of the fireplace opening, as I've described. Remarkably and luckily, the size of your test fire doesn't matter. Fireplaces never smoke because of the size of the fire but for other reasons like faulty geometry or sloppy construction. The good news is that your small test fire will tell you just as much as a big one and be much easier and safer to put out if it comes to that.

If your test fire works without smoking, congratulations! If it doesn't—if the chimney never drew all the smoke out—jump to Chapter III to find out about the aluminum foil tests.

THE PYRAMID FIRE

Most fireplace users, myself included for some 50 years, tend to lay their fires with the kindling and crunched up newspaper at the bottom, underneath the big logs or in between them, usually on andirons or a grate. We did this out of habit. Another style, which has become popular in the last 30 years, is exactly the reverse: the big logs are on the bottom, smaller split logs above in a crisscross pattern, and then kindling, maybe fire starter wafers and newspaper knots on top. It looks like a little pyramid. So the fire starts perhaps 10" to 20" above the hearth. The reason the top-down fire often works so well is that the newspaper knots, kindling, etc. heat up the chimney more quickly because they are higher in the firebox. They then start to burn and fall lower in the tower, setting the rest of the fuel on fire. The pyramid fire works best on a bed of ashes, not with a grate.

I would not recommend trying a top down fire unless you were familiar with the fireplace and knew that it was capable of working well. See Figure 7.

LAYING A PYRAMID OF FIRE

FIGURE 7

FIREPLACES FOR CELEBRATIONS

Fireplaces are always magnets at parties. People are naturally stimulated by well functioning fireplaces, just as their spirits are dampened by poorly functioning ones. And the more fireplaces you have burning at your party, the more excitement there will be in the air. I also believe that having two fireplaces burning in one space adds even greater excitement. The challenge at your Christmas party is keeping all these fireplaces well stocked with fuel. It wouldn't hurt to "appoint" selected willing guests to keep your home fires burning.

But a word to the wise: have a dry run without the guests, i.e., before the party with the multiple fireplaces in full swing. There can be a situation where the strongest fireplace(s) uses up so much air that the weaker, i.e., lower, fireplace chimneys become air intakes. Sometimes multiple fireplaces only work without smoking during cocktail holiday festivities because of the constant arrival and departure of guests, who open and shut the front door many, many times per hour, bringing in lots of outside air. (During your dry run, try cracking the front door a ½".)

One of the strategies that sometimes solves this problem is to make sure the basement has plenty of air, assuming it's not space that's being used for the party. More on air in CHAPTER III.

SUMMARY

Heat makes chimneys draw and more heat makes them draw harder. Glass doors are a valuable tool for heating a chimney. But after the chimney starts drawing—in a few minutes at most—glass doors should be opened for safety reasons. You're heating parts of the fireplace/chimney system not designed for lots of heat. Smoke plates and grates may also solve smoke problems by altering the ratio between the fireplace opening and the inside of the chimney. These are much cheaper than glass doors.

CHAPTER II

SWEEPS/BUILDERS: THE BIGGEST FIREPLACE SECRET

CONTENTS

The biggest secret, the missing piece—Rumford—How to execute after the fact—Can start at any depth, at the front or farther back—The Mermaid fireplace

My first 20 years as a chimney sweep/doctor were primarily spent solving smoke problems. I got so I could solve them all. But, even though I could stop the smoking, there were some 3% for which I couldn't explain the reason *why* they smoked. These fireplaces were in compliance with virtually all the fireplace design rules on record. When I was completely stymied, I'd just retreat to reducing the size of the fireplace opening, beyond what made sense, or, in a handful of cases, I'd resort to glass doors. I never did this willingly. I really wanted to understand the *cause* of the smoking. It felt like a cop-out if I didn't. (With *low* chimneys, which typically create *systemic smoking*, which is caused by lack of air in the house, I could solve virtually all of them with top dampers. More on this in Chapter III.)

My standard repertoire for structural problems included the following: reducing the size of the opening by lowering the top of the fireplace with a smoke plate or its equivalent (new masonry) or, very occasionally, closing in the sidewalls or raising the hearth; adding a true grate, as I described in Chapter I; taking out the back wall damper housing lip, which I describe in the next chapter. On many jobs I used a combination of these.

With greatly oversized fireboxes—way too big for an undersized flue—I would build an entirely new firebox inside the old firebox, bringing in the sidewalls and lowering the top. Raising the hearth was rare, a last resort.

Having fixed hundreds of smoking fireplaces—most of the time where others had tried and failed—I felt that I had so many tricks up my sleeve, I could solve any smoke problem.

THE MISSING PIECE

But exactly *why* those 3% of mystery fireplaces smoked continued to baffle me. *The missing link turned out to be the angle or splay of the sidewalls of the firebox.* You can read all the fireplace literature in the world—I have read way more than my share—and not learn or be informed *or realize that increasing the angle or splay of the sidewalls of a fireplace increases how hard its chimney draws and will solve (overwhelm!) almost any structural smoke problem.*

The power of splay is the biggest fireplace secret of all for solving structural smoke problems. Architects take note. (Structural smoking problems make up at least 60% of all smoking problems.)

While the splay angles found in Architectural Standard Graphics—these can be deduced from the recommended *dimensions* of fireplaces—are typically greater than 100 degrees, many fireplaces are built with even less. Some have no splay at all. I would like to save everyone a lot of grief and recommend increasing this angle to 115 degrees, especially if the design of the damper requires that it be installed at the same height as the top of the fireplace opening. The other condition requiring 115 degrees is if the damper, because of its design, cannot be installed all the way forward. As you can see from the illustration below, increasing the splay can be achieved by feathering one end of the brick and sawing the appropriate angle on the other end—so that each brick can fill in the back corner—or actually inserting the more angled brick into the sidewall. See Figure 8.

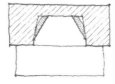

FEATHERED

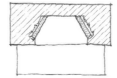

CHANNEL CUT INTO
THE SIDEWALL

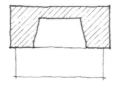

ORIGINAL FIREPLACE
(INADEQUATE SPLAY)

INCREASING SIDEWALL SPLAY

FIGURE 8

As you may recall, one of the reasons I believe a fireplace draws initially is because of the air pressure difference between the fireplace and the top of the chimney.

Increasing the splay increases the air pressure *on or near the back wall*, the hottest part of the fireplace and where most of the burning takes place. *My expanded explanation is that the pressure at and near the back wall is magnified by good splay.* During a fire increased pressure translates into more air, more oxygen, increased combustion, and, ultimately, most important of all, *more heat.* More heat means a hotter chimney and a hotter chimney means much harder draw.

These increases in air pressure and oxygen are modest, at least initially, but can make a big difference to the individual fireplace. I suspect they feed on themselves. What starts as modest pressure becomes greater as the chimney and firebox become hotter, making the drawing power increases exponential.

One way of thinking about this is that increased splay makes a fireplace behave more like a blast furnace.

SWEEP'S ROLE IN MAKING FIREPLACES BETTER
One of the general problems with fireplace design and construction is that builders and general contractors tend not to take fireplace innards—the firebox—seriously. They know how to make fireplaces look good on the outside with pleasing proportions, antique mantels, beautiful marble surrounds, and hearths but don't believe that the interior geometry and construction make much difference. As I mentioned in the introduction, they also believe that some fireplaces can never be made to work.

It has been my experience that chimney sweeps can play a major role here in the lives of people who love (or want to love!) their fireplaces and are rightfully demoralized and sometimes literally undone when they smoke. Entire building projects can be discredited because the fireplaces don't work. Sweeps reading this book need to realize they now have very valuable information at their fingertips. One day when I was correcting a smoking fireplace—I believe it had smoked for more than 150 years—at a fancy men's club in Washington, DC, a white-haired member stopped by to apologize to me for their terrible fireplace. I told him he needn't apologize at all because fixing flawed fireplaces were my bread-and-butter and, that, to the contrary, I was delighted that there was so much of this kind of work!

An especially good feature of increasing the splay is that the size and outer appearance of the fireplace are not altered or modified one iota. This is very important if the mantel and surround treatment need to be kept exactly the same, either to preserve the overall proportions or a decorative feature of stone or tile between the fireplace opening and the mantel.

Where better splay counts the most is when there are several *structural problems* that are, individually, very expensive or almost impossible to fix without ripping out the whole firebox and/or the whole chimney, and starting over. Examples might be the damper too low and/or too far back and a seriously incorrect ratio between the fireplace opening and the flue and several minor ledges, all of which, in the aggregate, create a major smoking problem. Even if these and other flaws are found in one fireplace, just increasing the splay can often overcome them all, a minor miracle in my opinion.

As you will see, however, fairly skilled brickwork is required for the installation or addition of new splay. When I build new splay, I have to saw more than half the new bricks, many with angles. I describe its execution in a moment.

To summarize the virtues of added splay, it's the one magic bullet in the world of smoking fireplaces. To count the ways: it is virtually unknown, it is always doable, and it is reliably effective. But, as I've said, best of all, *it is unobtrusive*, if given a light coat of black spray paint at the end of the job. (Otherwise, people would be tipped off by the new, smoke-free brickwork.)

I strongly prefer the undetectable or invisible fix.

While glass doors and smoke plates I described in the first chapter, are effective, they are obtrusive fixes.

INCREASING SPLAY PIONEERED BY RUMFORD

Although an extremely shallow fireplace can function without splay, it should have become a *sine qua non*—something which cannot be done without—for fireplace construction ever since it was first proposed and demonstrated in England by Count Rumford, an American-born scientist, over 200 years ago. The addition of splay was actually called Rumfordization in his day! Many American fireplaces, especially in grand houses in our antebellum south, were Rumfordized at that time. I have seen them in historic houses in Maryland, Virginia, South Carolina, and Florida and I'm certain there are many, many more.

Rumford, whom you'll read more about in Chapter V and Chapter IX, recommended splay of 135 degrees although less than that was acceptable. The British fireplaces Rumford made his reputation fixing at the end of the 18th century were typically square or rectangular on the inside without any splay at all.

The puzzling aspect of how Rumford's proposal was used and/or ignored is that few fireplace builders realized that increasing the angle of the splay of the sidewalls was the most important part of his proposal, *the part that prevented fireplaces from smoking.* Instead they treated it as an innovation that applied *solely* to Rumford-style fireplaces, not to all fireplaces—those already built or to be built. Indeed, I fault Rumford himself for not emphasizing that it was the increased splay that single-handedly and by itself prevented his fireplaces from smoking. Perhaps he did not fully grasp the effect of increased splay.

This misunderstanding of the power of splay was worse in the US. As you will see in Chapter IX, the British grasped it fairly quickly. For myself, I had splayed the sidewalls of fireplaces for many years before I understood its function. I did it because the housing of the cast iron damper I was using was angled 110 degrees so I simply extended that angle. See Figure 9.

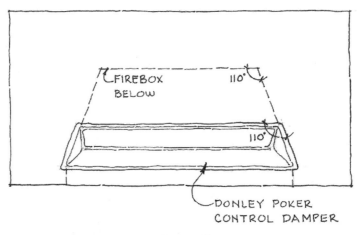

REAR

FRONT

DAMPER HOUSING ANGLE

FIGURE 9

It made intuitive sense to do it that way and I liked how it looked—the angled walls were more beautiful. It's only been since 1999 that I grasped the significant technical impact. To me, fireplace splay is one of the great examples of the confluence of form and function.

Later in this chapter, I describe how I finally saw the light—what splay really did.

The second most important part of the Rumford design, narrowing the throat depth to 4", reduces house air loss and cooling of the rest of the house. This is a flaw intrinsic to all fireplaces but which is made somewhat less bad by the 4" restriction. In Chapter V, I show how to restrict a hot chimney far more and make any fireplace into a real heater.

When I am confronted with splay of 100 degrees or less in a smoking fireplace, I aim for new splay between 115 and 120 degrees, 110 as *the absolute minimum*. To determine these angles, you have to have a bevel and protractor or speed square and small square. (For professionals or for those who like gadgets, I strongly recommend a battery-powered *digital angle meter. Once you figure out how to use it, it saves you lots of time*.) See Figure 10.

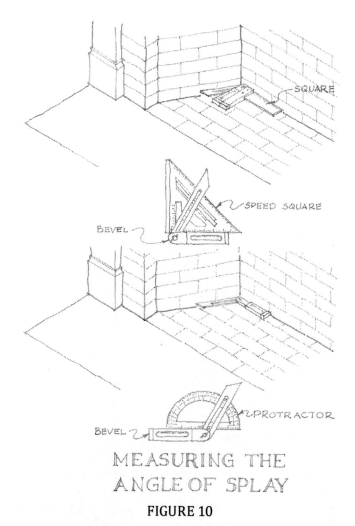

MEASURING THE
ANGLE OF SPLAY

FIGURE 10

I measure the old splay and decide, based on the particulars of each fireplace, how much (more) splay I need. I then draw out the new trapezoid shape on the hearth as a guide to the geometry for the new fireplace. See Figure 11.

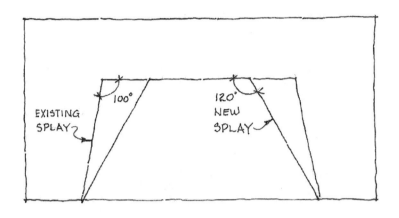

LAYING OUT
NEW SPLAY
ON HEARTH

FIGURE 11

The illustration below presents an idea of some of the possibilities. I've included the 135-degree trapezoid recommended by Rumford even though most modern Rumford-style fireplaces, with the occasional exception, sport splay of 120 or 125 degrees. (Notice that 135-degree splay calls for a much shallower firebox to attain even a modestly usable width at the back wall.) I have seen fireplaces that work without smoking that are only 100 degrees but that is rare. Most fireplaces range between 100 and

110 degrees. I've named one of the splays by its original damper manufacturer, Donley, the very important but now bankrupt damper company I discuss in Chapter IX. See Figure 12.

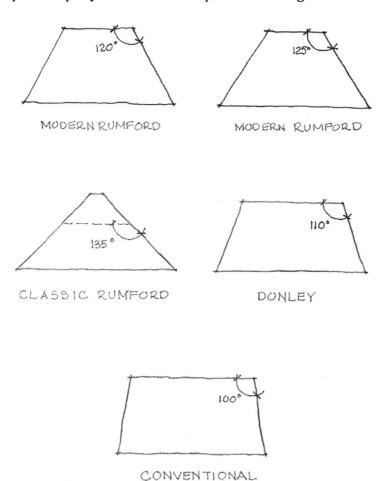

HEARTH SPLAY ANGLES

FIGURE 12

The ideal geometric shape for the inner hearth is, as you can see, a fairly *severe* trapezoid. It has been my experience that increasing splay starting from the arbitrary baseline of 100 degrees increases fireplace drawing strength roughly 1 to 2% for each additional degree. Most structural smoking constitutes less than 8% of the total smoke made by the fire. So, increasing the splay, even only modestly, 5 to 10 degrees, can thus solve most structural smoking. See upper half of drawing with different possible splays in Figure 13.

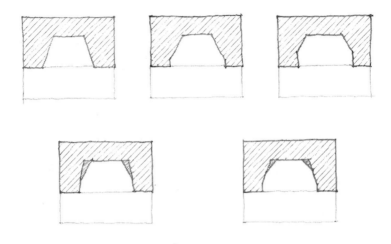

DIFFERENT SPLAY
POSSIBILITIES

FIGURE 13

A surprising feature of increasing the splay of the sidewalls is that you can add it starting virtually *anywhere* on the sidewalls, starting all the way at the front, 4" in, ½ the way in or even the last 6". In every case, it does the job. In fact, to solve a slight but lingering smoke problem in a fireplace I'd just built from scratch, I added what I now call *back splay* to 110 degree splay, effectively taking out the back corners. This small change strengthened the fireplace enough so that it now worked perfectly. See lower half of drawing above.

The way I usually increase the splay is to cut channels a full firebrick wide right behind the front half brick end, which starts the sidewall. Because I change the fireplace splay in *existing homes where people are living*, making a channel with my masonry saw would create far too much dust. Instead, I cut the old sidewall brick by drilling a line of holes with my masonry drill and then angling the bit up and down through the holes. I can then cut it the rest of the way with a masonry chisel. As the illustration shows, I only have to cut every other brick because every other brick is a full brick and can be removed whole. See Figure 14.

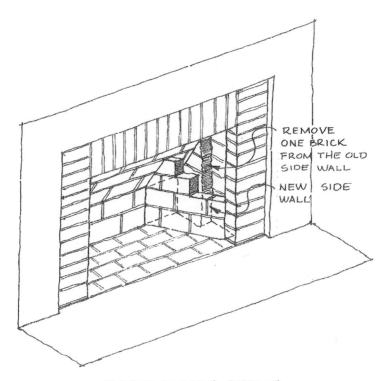

REMOVE ONE BRICK FROM THE OLD SIDE WALL

NEW SIDE WALL

BUILDING NEW SIDE WALL SPLAY
FIGURE 14

When I build new splay, I always use refractory cement because it makes the side walls more stable, a real necessity where the new splay butts the back wall, an area of great heat. I also work diligently to keep my mortar joints tight by sawing bricks to meet the angles the splay makes with the back wall. My joints on the horizontal are less than 1/16 inch and usually less than 1/8 inch on the vertical. Such small and therefore strong joints are only possible with refractory cement.

Shorter firewood is often called for with new splay, especially with average-sized fireplaces, if we are laying the wood parallel to or against the back wall. *Firewood should not be longer than the back wall is wide.* Wood suppliers can usually accommodate customers, within reason. They often have shorter *stove-length* firewood available. (For the record, Count Rumford was altering *coal-burning* fireplaces. Most of the 19th century American Rumfordizations I have seen have reduced the recommended 135-degree splay to 120 so that the back wall could be sufficiently wide for burning 2-foot long wood. Thomas Jefferson may have been one of the first to do this when he designed the fireplaces at Monticello.)

In relatively narrow fireplaces, even splay of 110 degrees makes the back wall too short to hold normal-length firewood. If you have a narrow back wall, the only way you can burn normal sized logs is teepee style with the logs on end leaning against the back wall. And, of course, if you have also angled or pitched the back wall much, the teepee style is not practical. See my solution below.

THE MERMAID FIREPLACE

When modifying these narrow fireplaces, I've experimented with a *mermaid design*, so named by me because the floor of the firebox—the mermaid's tail, as it were—is much wider than the top, her head. For example, with a fireplace 28" or 26" wide and 16" deep, you can hardly introduce any splay without reducing the back wall to way less than 2'. (Or else greatly reducing its depth.) I solve this by a process of progressive cantilevering— adding steps of splay. I start the firebox almost square or 2' wide on the back wall. After laying 9" of firebrick (two courses on edge), I start to splay *the side walls* an inch on each side with each course, the back wall will gradually become less wide and the angle at the top of the fireplace great enough to prevent smoking. I stop increasing the splay one brick course (4.5") below the damper. (Remember the kind of smoking we're talking about here is structural not systemic, i.e., caused by lack of air in the house.) If house air is moving with increased pressure into the *top of the fireplace opening*—the only site we ever see for structural smoking and the kind of smoking we're trying to prevent here— it's almost impossible for smoke to spill out. See Figure 15.

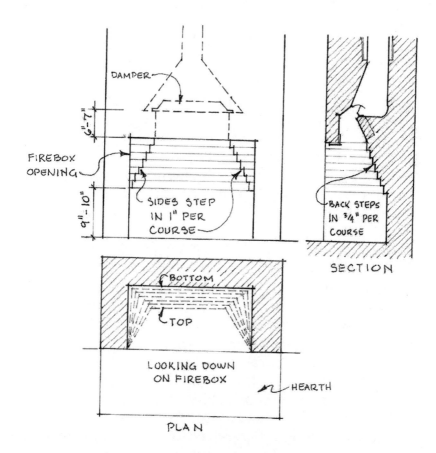

THE MERMAID FIREPLACE

FIGURE 15

For the record, classic Rumfordizations done 200 years ago that feature a narrow leg or post on each side of the fireplace opening of 1" to 3", indicating that the newly splayed walls were simply *added without inserting them* into the old sidewall. I only do this if I think the whole box also needs to be smaller, less wide. The new splay in these 200-year old fireplaces is typically parged, i.e., coated smooth with mortar or plaster and painted white with a lime wash, per Rumford's instructions.

To give you an idea how few of even the best fireplace mechanics understand the power of splay to solve smoking, I have seen only 2 attempts at solving mysterious smoke problems by *increasing the splay*. I'm making the assumption that the increased splay, 120 degrees, had been done because of persistent smoke problems. Both fireplaces were in large expensive mansions. From their location in the houses—and the décor of the rooms they were located in—I could tell these were the fireplaces the owners most wanted to use. The other fireplaces in the house had not been altered. I further assumed that only the most experienced fireplace mechanics did the work because of the superb quality of the brickwork. Regular bricklayers hate working on their knees in a confined space.

Unfortunately, their fine work was for naught. One smoking problem was actually caused by a slightly short chimney, the other by a serious lack of air throughout the entire house. Increasing the splay in these cases, of course, created no improvement because these were *systemic smoking problems,* a different kind of smoking, which I explain in the next chapter. Increasing the splay only solves structural problems.
In both cases, what struck me was the unusually good splay, which I'd only seen on classic Rumfords. (A possible scenario here is that there were both kinds of smoking, structural and systemic. The improved splay solved the structural smoking but not the systemic.)

The other unusual feature was that *the entire fireboxes* had been rebuilt, a perfectly legitimate and, in some cases, a preferable option to only increasing the splay, especially if there is also a damper lip, incorrect mortar, and overall instability in the original brickwork. Only rebuilding the splay, however, and not the whole firebox, is significantly less expensive and suffices in 90% of these cases.

Only about 30% of the fireplaces built today have even moderately adequate splay. This is a design problem—architects and builders simply do not *understand its functional importance* in preventing smoking.

THE MOMENT I DISCOVERED THE POWER OF SPLAY

I think I'd been circling around this possibility subconsciously for some years. What may happen when you are immersed in something—anything, I suppose—for a long time, that curious part of your brain is always trying, *below the level of your normal consciousness,* to make sense of the whole thing, to puzzle it out. Early on, I remember being mystified why a particular fireplace in Philadelphia—not one I'd built—simply didn't draw reliably. I studied it carefully. The only difference I noticed from the hundreds of fireplaces I'd built was that the sidewalls were less splayed. (I still had not begun actually measuring the angle in degrees. But I can now estimate with some confidence that it was a little more than 100 degrees whereas it should have been at least 110 degrees.)

It was during this time when I was experimenting with stepping the back wall of the fireplace to increase heat output, which worked great. So I was already involved in tweaking the inside of fireboxes. And I continued to read and reread Count Rumford's famous paper.

And then, out of the clear blue, a fortuitous event took place in 1999. Believe it or not I was in Estonia—one of the countries bordering the Baltic Sea, which includes Denmark, Sweden, Poland, Finland, Latvia, and Lithuania—where my son Jake was working as on-site manager of an American recycling company. To entertain his old man, Jake had set up a meeting with some local fireplace people, 4 young men in their 20's. We were in a neighborhood bar sitting at a table. There was a fireplace in the corner about 10 feet away. The small amount of wood in it was just smoldering. It was a spring evening.

Communication was difficult. Jake is fluent in Russian, which is partly why he got the job. (About a third of Estonia's population is Russian.) Only one of the 4 young Estonians spoke much Russian and Jake knows almost no Estonian, an even more difficult language than Russian. Of course, I know neither. Jake would have to translate my questions into Russian to the young man who knew some Russian and he would have to translate that into Estonian for his associates. Answers would have to come back along that same avenue. When they would ask me a question, the process would reverse.

It was pretty heavy going. I think I may have got a little drunk. Suddenly, out of the blue, I was drawing on a napkin how I personally solved fireplace smoke problems—*increasing the splay, the angle of the sidewalls*. I had asked the Estonians how they solved smoke problems. They had just shrugged. *I'd never before thought of what I was telling them until that very moment.* I'd never even considered it. before then. Yet, at that moment, I believed that I was right on target. I knew it in my bones.

In hindsight, it seems obvious. After all, the angle of the sidewalls is one of the grossest variables in fireplace construction. I must have been subconsciously trying to puzzle this out for many years—what was splay for, what did it actually do, was it done just for the looks, etc. That it could solve a smoking problem was such a radical idea that I couldn't access it until I was drunk in the company of people who probably didn't even understand what I was getting at and whom I knew I would very likely never see again. I remember Jake being a little annoyed with me when we left the bar. He was familiar with my fireplace work and yet had never before heard of increasing the splay as a means to cure smoking. He may also have been a little disgusted that I'd got drunk and made a bad impression.

As far as I'm concerned, three cheers to visiting a really, really foreign country, having a few beers, and sharing about your work! This was transformative, a real breakthrough for me.

Shortly after returning to Washington I had two jobs, which went beyond my usual repertoire of fixes. The first was an old fireplace that had just been refaced with beautiful ochre-veined marble. It had no proper smoke chamber leading up to the flue. Instead, there was an undersized *horizontal* channel about 4' long which fed at a right angle into the chimney. Additionally, its damper was only 2 inches above the fireplace opening when it should have been at least 5". Obviously, the fireplace smoked like crazy.

I described the hopelessness of the situation to the homeowner and said there was only one fix I could think of that did not entail massive reconstruction—the creation of a smoke chamber above the fireplace and alteration to the front. Or glass doors. And that was to increase the splay up to around 125 degrees. (It was currently about 105 degrees.) And I couldn't guarantee it would solve such a severe smoking problem.

He said no to the glass doors but to go ahead and give the increased splay a try. I then had to figure out exactly how to increase splay in the most cost effective way. The method I came up with is almost identical to the method I use today. (I described how I do it a few pages ago.) This first attempt of mine actually succeeded! Additionally, the fireplace became an incredible heater because so little house air was also pulled up the chimney, just enough air to prevent smoking.

A couple weeks later, I solved another smoking problem with increased splay, taking it from 100 degrees to 115 degrees. This was in a tall row house. The fireplace was 30" x 30". A 6" stainless steel liner had been installed, making the ratio between the flue liner and fireplace opening almost one to 30. I think the reasons it worked once I'd increased the splay were that the chimney was very tall—more than 40', interior, and lined with that stainless steel which heats up instantly.

Anyway, after these two jobs I was hooked.

I am amazed how circuitous my route was to grasping the significance of splay. A very early job I did involved adding splay of about 125 degrees to a fireplace whose damper was too short and creating 4-inch wide ledge (or roof) on each side of the throat. I took out the existing sidewalls and added the splay *out of necessity* to take out the ledges, not to increase the splay per se. I kept the fireplace width the same. (I had not yet grasped that splay could affect smoking.) The fireplace was 36" wide and 28" high. I had assumed before I did the work that the flue liner was 9" X 13" or 77" square on the inside, the size flue you'd expect for this size fireplace. When I tested it, after increasing the splay, it worked perfectly. And then I just happened to notice that the flue was actually 9"X 9", less than 50" square on the inside. If you do the math, the ratio was around 1 to 20, simply impossible, I believed at the time, for a smoke-free fireplace. I assumed, however, that this had to be an anomaly. I had not yet grasped that all fireplaces are subject to real, hard-and-fast laws. I could have saved myself more than some 15 years if I'd taken this fireplace seriously!

SUMMARY

The degree of splay of a fireplace can determine whether it smokes. Splay can be changed on existing fireplaces, unobtrusively and without changing the size of the fireplace opening. Each degree increase in splay increases the draw between one and 2 percent. Splay has never before been acknowledged in anything written about fireplaces—books or architectural manuals—to affect smoking, with the exception of one weak reference by Rumford. See Chapter IX.

CHAPTER III

FOR ARCHITECTS: SYSTEMIC SMOKING

CONTENTS

Top dampers start low chimneys on one-story additions—Top dampers block cold air and makes flue warmer—Systemic smoking caused by lack of air—Nature abhors vacuum—Systemic and structural smoke often exist together—Chimneys draw combination of smoke and house air—Chimney effect—Airtight houses—Challenging job required exhaust fan—Insulating exterior chimney flues at the outset—Interior fireplace systems rarely have systemic problems—Rules for architects, 5 structural, 3 systemic

I was in the basement. The homeowner yelled to me that the fireplace down there was completely plugged. He'd tried to use it. It wouldn't draw.

I opened the damper. Cold air streamed down into my face. The chimney was wide open. There was no blockage.

What was happening is that this basement fireplace was acting as an air intake because the basement was starved for air, the usual condition of most basements.

Systemic smoking is a very different kind of problem from structural smoking, which is always caused by design or construction flaws at the fireplace itself. These flaws partially obstruct or slow down the flow of smoke up the chimney. This basement fireplace had no flaws at all. In fact, an identical fireplace on the first floor above worked perfectly. The reason this fireplace was not drawing was solely caused by its location in the system—the basement.

A Fireplace May Work in One House and Not in Another
Because a fireplace works in one house is no guarantee that one with the exact same design will work in another. The case I have in mind was the mastermind of a smart architect in Washington, DC. The family had a country place with a wonderful fireplace, which worked to perfection: it started drawing immediately, never smoked, drew reliably throughout the fire, was immune to changes in wind or weather, never smelled even on the rainiest days or weeks, etc. When they added an addition to their house in Washington, they replicated their country fireplace exactly: same size opening, same size flue liner, same chimney height, same geometry inside the firebox, same damper positioned the same way, the same in every way they could think of.

It never worked very well. The difference, it turned out, was that the house system within which it was located was different. Specifically, in this case, it came down to the difference in the height of the rest of the house. In the country, the fireplace chimney was the tallest point of their house. In Washington, it was about 6 feet lower than two taller chimneys. One of the oldest (I think, unwritten) rules of fireplace/chimney design is that all fireplace chimneys should be the same height and the tallest part of the house.

Distinguishing between systemic and structural smoking is easy. Structural smoking only takes place at *the top of the fireplace opening, as I've said,* and can be fixed with a smoke plate. It is predictable. Usually, only a small portion of the smoke—no more than 8%—being generated by the fire will seep out. Systemic smoking, on the other hand, is random and changing, typically entails much more smoke, and can be harder to fix because its cause always lies beyond the fireplace itself. What can be truly bewildering is when both kinds of smoking exist together, which makes all of this so much more fun! See Figure 16.

STRUCTURAL SMOKING

SYSTEMIC SMOKING

TWO MAIN KINDS OF SMOKING

FIGURE 16

THE ADDITION FIREPLACE

An even more common type of systemic smoking than the basement fireplace occurs with a fireplace on a one-story addition to a multi-storied house. Its low chimney, like that of the basement fireplace chimney, has also become an air intake, in this case because its chimney is shorter than the rest of the taller old house and much shorter than its other chimneys. See Figure 17.

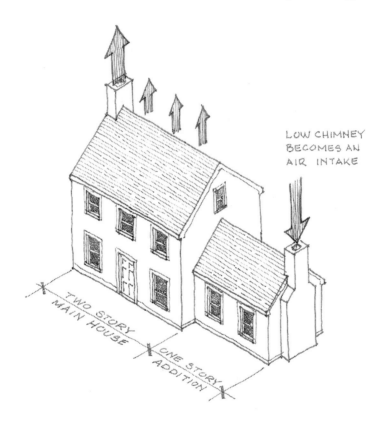

LOW CHIMNEY

FIGURE 17

Systemic smoking illustrates the principle that Nature Abhors a Vacuum, which actually translates into Nature Always Seeks

Equal Air Pressure. If the air pressure at a fireplace is lower than the air pressure at the top of the chimney, the result is systemic smoking.

There are two strategies for fixing these fireplaces with these problems: glass doors and the top damper. I described how to use glass doors in the first chapter.

The top damper is usually a better—less expensive—choice for the addition fireplace. Unlike the traditional, low at the throat of the fireplace, it is at the top of the chimney. Its controls are attached to a sidewall of the firebox, a stainless steel cable inside the flue connecting the controls to a movable door at the top of the chimney. See Figure 18.

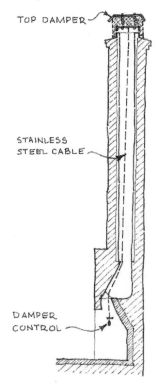

THE TOP DAMPER

FIGURE 18

What the top damper does while in the closed position (i.e., before a fire is lit) is to block the rush of cold air down the low chimney and to set up a modest circulation system of warm air from the house rising up through the open regular throat damper to the top of the short chimney. The air gives up some heat, is cooled, and falls back into the house. When you open the top damper to light a fire, two things have changed: cold air is not streaming down the short chimney and the chimney itself is somewhat warm. See Figure 19.

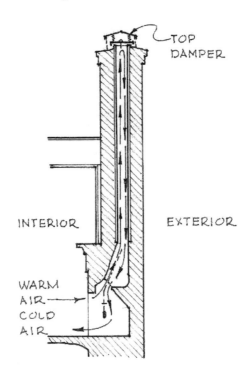

THE TOP DAMPER
ON A LOW CHIMNEY
FIGURE 19

STARTING A LOW CHIMNEY FIREPLACE USING A TOP DAMPER

1. *Lay the makings of a very small fire with lots of kindling so there will be real heat in the chimney almost immediately.*
2. *Crack a window nearby.*
3. *Open the top damper and determine that no outside air is coming down the chimney into the house. (If air is coming down, try heating the flue with a newspaper torch or two. If air continues coming down, quit.)*
4. *Only light the fire when the chimney has started drawing.*
5. *Add more small pieces of firewood and finally, when there's a vigorous smoke-free fire, bigger logs.*

Never shy away from showing the homeowner these steps by actually building a fire. You will make a friend for life! Architects and chimney sweeps take note.

The main point to take away from systemic smoking is that for a fireplace to work correctly, it must always be drawing a *combination of smoke from the fire and air from the house.* Many people assume that chimneys can magically distinguish between smoke and air and only draw the former. Even if there is no fire in the fireplace and the damper is open or, if closed, just leaking a little, the chimney, in the best of worlds, will be drawing. (Sometimes, a fireplace system seems neutral. It's neither drawing nor is outside air coming down. Adding just a little heat in these cases almost always starts it drawing.)

AIR PRESSURE IN MULTI-LEVEL HOUSES

How air is distributed in a multi-level house creates systemic smoking. In the winter there is always more air—greater air pressure—on the top floors of a house than outside and less air than outside in the lower part of the house. This condition is almost universal during the heating season. For instance, when you open a first floor or basement door to the outside, you feel a blast of cold air coming into the house. On the other hand, when you open a window on the second floor, you feel nothing because it is warm house air flowing out of the house. The resulting phenomenon is caused by the "chimney effect" because it mirrors what normally happens in a chimney—warm air, smoke, and gasses rise, incidentally creating lower air pressure below. See Figure 20.

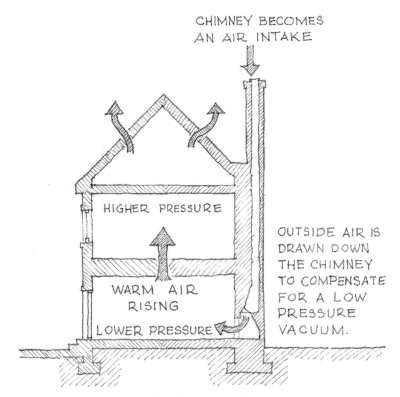

CHIMNEY BECOMES
AN AIR INTAKE

HIGHER PRESSURE

OUTSIDE AIR IS
DRAWN DOWN
THE CHIMNEY
TO COMPENSATE
FOR A LOW
PRESSURE
VACUUM.

WARM AIR
RISING

LOWER PRESSURE

A TIGHTLY SEALED HOUSE
CREATES A SHORTAGE
OF OUTSIDE AIR (VACUUM)

TIGHT BUILDING
ENVELOPE

FIGURE 20

If we didn't live in (more or less) airtight houses designed to conserve heat, there would be no problem. Outside air would always be flowing into the lower part of our houses. Making them more or less airtight has made the chimney, especially the low chimney, the path of least resistance for outside air to enter many houses.

ONE OF MY MOST CHALLENGING JOBS

While the top damper strategy is almost always effective, one job I had was much more extreme. For starters, the house was much larger and much taller than other ones I had worked on with short chimneys. It was very grand, with wonderfully high ceilings. The new kitchen/family room addition with its new fireplace, however, had a new, short chimney. There were many other fireplaces on the 1st and 2nd floors, original ones with tall chimneys. (There was even an auxiliary gas furnace on the third floor, which was also drawing air out of the house!) It seemed that there were chimneys everywhere and, of course, all much taller than the new short chimney. Most of the fireplace dampers were also open—this is usually the case—or, even when closed, leaking badly. After a few years in the chimney business, you register almost without thinking just how much air and air pressure there is in a house and how much of a deficit. Even before I entered the new kitchen/family room with the new fireplace, I had become dubious about solving their smoking problem, which had been described over the phone in the most lurid terms, using my usual method, the top damper, and maybe some outside air intakes. Inside air, I suspected, was in extremely short supply.

Even with the regular throat damper closed, I could sense that there was cold air flowing out of the new fireplace at a good rate, obviously leaking around the damper plate.

But when I actually opened this damper, the rush of outside air was a surprise even to a jaded professional like myself. It was a veritable torrent. This big old house was starved for air, literally. Given these extreme conditions, I knew beyond a shadow of a doubt that a top damper alone would not be strong enough to do this job. I had mentioned glass doors early on—a legitimate solution, especially if combined with a top damper—only to have the homeowners reject the doors out of hand for cosmetic reasons.

One of my early recommendations was to get more air into the boiler room in the basement below. The basement-located natural gas-fired central heater had the typically tall chimney. Additionally, its cross-sectional area was 3 times bigger than necessary. I described the situation to the builder, noting that this was a problem with many big old houses. A few days later he called back and said they'd put in an outside air intake, as I'd instructed. I was delighted until I saw it. Instead of being 6" in diameter, the minimum I'd recommended, it was 3/4th"! Even a sophisticated builder proved to be very naïve about how much a big, tall, hot chimney can draw. I also suspect he just did not like the idea of a big intake into the small enclosed boiler room. I have noticed that most people don't take air and air pressure seriously because they can't see them.

Another suggestion I made was to use a small basement room on an outside wall as an intake staging area where outside air could be warmed by a thermostatically activated electric heater before entering the basement proper. The homeowner rejected this, I think because it seemed too complicated to him. What I had imagined is that getting significantly more air into the house system at large would mean a top damper alone might be able to do the job.

Instead, I was reduced to a narrow solution, only involving the fireplace chimney. Much against my principles, I installed a powerful *exhaust fan*—something I had never been forced to do before because I could always figure out another way to solve this kind of problem. (Along with the fan, I installed a top damper to prevent cold air from leaking into the house when *the fireplace was not in use.*) See Figure 21.

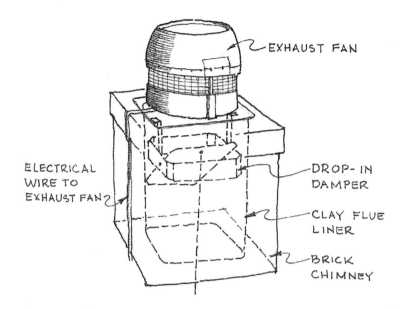

ELECTRICAL
WIRE TO
EXHAUST FAN

EXHAUST FAN

DROP-IN
DAMPER

CLAY FLUE
LINER

BRICK
CHIMNEY

EXHAUST FAN
WITH DROP-IN
TOP DAMPER

FIGURE 21

It worked! The fireplace could be used without smoking, the fan was easy enough to operate—the control switch at the fireplace included several speeds—and it didn't create any specific problems. The top damper successfully stopped most of the influx of cold air when the fireplace was not in use. Again, as we have seen with all the solutions to this particular problem that I have offered so far, I had not had any of my proposals accepted to actually help *fix the problem*. All I been allowed to do is overwhelm it. For instance, if I'd been able to get significantly more air into this big old house, I could say I'd *fixed* at least some of the problem. In practice, I have found this is usually impossible to do, mainly because it's in conflict with preconceptions or prejudices that most homeowners have.

At this particular job the contractor, on my recommendation, put in two outside air intakes, one on each side of the fireplace. (I describe these particular intakes in a moment.)

Speaking of *low* chimneys, one of the main causes of systemic smoking, you might ask, why not just make these low chimneys taller? Sometimes they are arbitrarily made shorter because the architect likes that look and some chimneys could indeed be made taller. But the usual problem is that these chimneys serve fireplaces in additions, which are less tall than the rest of the house. The problem of raising the chimney then becomes one of stability. A strong gust of wind could blow them over. Building codes in most jurisdictions call for chimneys not to exceed the structure they serve by more than 10 feet. So it's very rare that an addition chimney can legally (and safely) be made as tall as the other chimneys on an existing house. Even if you add significant height, if they are still not as tall as the other chimneys, they will continue to act as air intakes although less powerful ones. At this particular job, the top of the new chimney was some 20 feet below the tops of the old chimneys. We weren't even close.

To return to chimney exhaust fans for a moment, these are similar to glass doors in that they can solve *both structural and systemic smoking problems*. But they employ, as you saw, quite different means. Doors harness *the power of heat* to make a flawed system operate. Exhaust fans simply overwhelm the flawed system with mechanical force. The two really exist in separate worlds. Both must also be used, in different ways, at the end of a fire to insure no smoke at all and no odor: doors must be closed, probably also closing the air intakes at the bottom of the frame, and fans must be left on all night although at lower speed. This latter practice is wasteful on two fronts: electricity must be used and lots of heated house air is inevitably also pulled up the chimney and thrown away. When you'd most like to use a fireplace, say during an electrical blackout when even your boiler or furnace can't function, a low-chimney fireplace with a top damper (or glass doors) to facilitate start-up is still operable while a fan-driven fireplace obviously is not.

I've described *after-the-fact* solutions to the problem of low chimneys: top dampers, outside air intakes, glass doors, and exhaust fans. In serious cases, as we saw with the big old house, more than one of these may be necessary.

If an exhaust fan is the solution, outside air intakes of some kind are also almost always necessary so as to not (further) depressurize the house. (Boiler or furnace chimneys may stop functioning reliably and safely: pilot lights may go out and chimneys stop drawing 100%.) Glass doors, or better yet, top dampers, are necessary to prevent serious downdrafts when the fireplace is not in use. For a top damper to work really well in this application, it should be able to close completely. Some top damper designs fall a little short in this department.

As I've said, I would only consider exhaust fans as a last resort. They are expensive to purchase and they can be expensive to install.

MORE ON TOP DAMPERS

While top dampers can play a very important role in solving systemic fireplace smoking, there are details about them you should be aware of. To review, top dampers are installed on the top of chimneys and are controlled by means of a stainless steel cable connected to bracket that is mounted on the sidewall of the fireplace. Most controls feature a 6" to 8" length of ball chain or regular chain at the end of the cable, which is threaded through the bracket. See Figure 22.

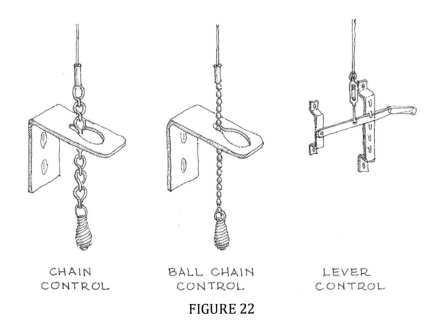

CHAIN CONTROL   BALL CHAIN CONTROL   LEVER CONTROL

FIGURE 22

Most of the dampers themselves are more or less flat plates, which go up and down vertically according to the control setting at the firebox. There are also swivel or pivot dampers and a butterfly design. For drawings of a selection of top dampers, see Figure 23.

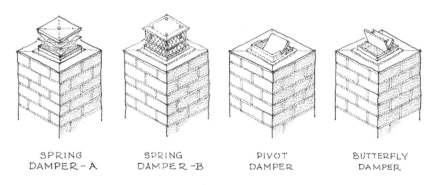

SPRING DAMPER - A   SPRING DAMPER - B   PIVOT DAMPER   BUTTERFLY DAMPER

FIGURE 23

All top dampers are spring-loaded open or, if on a pivot, heavier on one side of the pivot than the other and therefore weighted open. The cable's only function, with the exception of one style of damper, is *to close or restrict the damper*, not to open it.

Assuming that your fireplace already has a regular (throat) damper, I strongly recommend that the stainless steel cable be routed *through the front housing* of the throat damper so that you end up with two working dampers. My reasoning is that most throat dampers leak a little—because of the high temperatures, there is no gasket, just metal on metal—so two dampers are appropriate from the point of view of energy conservation. But having two dampers also serves a very important function on exterior chimneys, which perhaps make up appropriately 80% of all chimneys built in the last 100 years. This is because even with the top damper closed, hot air from the house goes up the chimney to the top damper, is cooled and falls back down into the house. A closed throat damper greatly reduces this action and conserves house heat. See Figure 24.

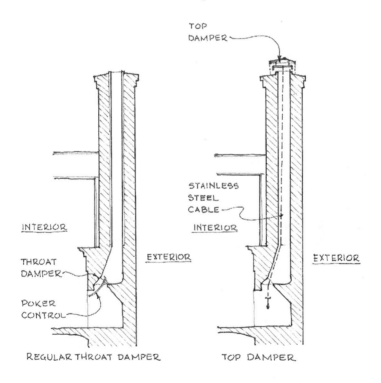

TWO TYPES OF DAMPERS

FIGURE 24

(If the top damper is on a *low* chimney, you *may want* to open the throat damper an hour or so before lighting the fire so the chimney warms up better. More on this in Chapter V.)

Here are directions for installing top damper cables:
Routing the cable through the throat damper housing is fairly simple because most dampers are made of low-grade cast iron, which is relatively soft. I first drill a pilot hole with a 1/8" drill bit at one side of the top of the housing and then, if I'm using the short piece of protective cable sleeve, enlarge the hole. If I misfire and the damper can't open and close without hitting the cable, I drill another, better located hole. The whole job, once you're up to speed, shouldn't take more than five minutes. See Figure 25.

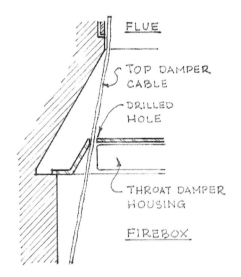

FLUE

TOP DAMPER CABLE

DRILLED HOLE

THROAT DAMPER HOUSING

FIREBOX

ROUTING THE TOP DAMPER CABLE
THROUGH THE THROAT DAMPER HOUSING

ROUTING THE TOP DAMPER CABLE
FIGURE 25

Speaking of cable sleeves, these can create problems, I assume by rusting slightly on the inside between the stainless cable and the sleeve and creating lots of friction during opening and closing the damper. This is especially true of a long run. It is my impression that sleeves are probably unnecessary because stainless steel cable is more or less indestructible. See CHAPTER V for more discussion of top dampers and CHAPTER XI for suppliers.

I find it irresponsible to install a top damper and throw away the throat damper plate, which has been the practice of almost all top damper installers. While this might make some sense if the top damper cable could *only* be routed through the damper opening, rerouting the cable is strongly preferable. It's useful to remember that, if the top damper is being installed to solve a structural smoking problem, it is almost never the *throat damper plate* itself that is causing the smoking but its damper housing. (See Chapter IV for correcting ledges made by throat damper housing.)

OTHER SYSTEMIC SMOKING PROBLEMS

Systemic smoking drives several unrelated phenomena. These include when *fireplace use* lowers the air pressure in the house (or in a small room) so much that the chimney becomes an air intake. Basement fireplaces typically have systemic smoking problems because of low air pressure in basements. Three other instances, which I describe later, are wind-caused downdrafts with fireplaces, fireplace odors, and malfunctioning hot air furnace returns.

Remember how I explained what makes fireplace chimneys draw initially? It's the difference in air pressure, less at the top of the chimney than at the bottom. With systemic smoking, this dynamic has been reversed: greater pressure at the top of the chimney or, put another way, reduced pressure at the fireplace.

If, when you open the damper, air blows down into your face, you have a systemic problem. Some systemic problems are minor, as I've mentioned, and cracking a window before lighting the fire will do the trick. Adding a little heat may also help turn the tide, as I've mentioned. More serious systemic smoking requires more.

One of the most surprising solutions to a systemic smoking problem featured two fireplaces served by different chimneys, one interior and one exterior, about 16 feet apart. Both fireplaces were built correctly—good ratio, good splay, no ledges, proper damper placement, chimneys the same height. But the fireplace with the exterior chimney was unreliable: sometimes it worked fine without smoking, sometimes not. What made the difference, I figured out, was whether the interior fireplace damper was left open or closed. Left open, the interior chimney would draw hard enough to make the exterior chimney become an outside air intake. And this was without a fire in the interior fireplace! The problem was made worse, of course, with a fire. If the interior fireplace's damper was closed, the exterior fireplace worked fine. Do remember that interior chimneys are always stronger than exterior chimneys!

For the record, many smoking fireplaces, as I mentioned earlier, have *both* structural and systemic components. Ooh-la-la!

OUTSIDE AIR-INTAKES

To reduce systemic smoking, the building codes of many local jurisdictions now require outside air intakes for new fireplace construction.

There are three basic kinds of intakes. The first kind adds outside air right inside the firebox itself. A three-inch round pipe is installed in the back or sidewalls of the firebox. Another kind of intake is a larger boot installed into the inner hearth, which introduces the air at the front of the firebox floor. Both of these can be closed after a fashion.

Neither of them ever worked very well for me, although the larger boot worked a little. The 3-inch one completely inside the firebox worked the least well even though the smoking was obviously being caused by lack of air.

I finally realized that air *inside* the firebox was only a small part of what was needed to prevent the smoking. How it helped a little was to (eventually) increase *the air pressure* inside the fireplace, a very good thing. What was more important, however, was *air pressure at large* in the room with the fireplace. Partly what prevents a fireplace from smoking is house air *sweeping into the firebox*, which prevents smoke from spilling out. Introducing air beyond the firebox does two things: maintains the integrity of the *wall of air* flowing into the firebox and increases firebox air pressure.

Fireplace systems partly need air to drive the chimney, i.e., to prevent smoking. If we assume that 1/3 to 1/2 of what is going up the hot chimney is *house air pure and simple*, and I believe it is higher than 1/2 in many systems, you can see that you would indeed need lots and lots of air. (I suspect that the amount of house air drawn up the chimney with the smoke varies to some extent with the air pressure available inside the house.)

Experimentation is the only fool-proof way to determine how much air is needed, first to start the fireplace chimney and then, when it becomes hot, to keep it going.

Chimneys work initially, as I've described, because of a difference in air pressure at the bottom of the chimney and at the top. Having little air (pressure) at the bottom of the chimney ignores the most basic chimney requirement.

I should note here that *completely interior* fireplaces and chimneys almost never have *systemic* smoking problems because the whole chimney is always warm. This is proof that insulating exterior chimneys, which I describe in Chapter IV, should prevent or, at a minimum, greatly reduce this kind of smoking.

THE CONDAR

The best outside air intake I know of is made by Condar. It closes quite well, unlike the inside-the-fireplace intakes which tend to leak badly even when closed. It is 4" in diameter with an area of 12" square, almost double the capacity of the smaller 3" inside-the-fireplace intakes, which have an area of about 7" square. See Figure 26.

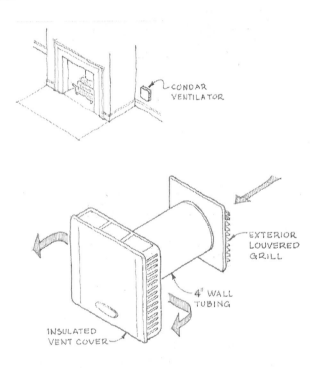

CONDAR
AIR SUPPLY VENTILATOR

FIGURE 26

The Condar was designed to supply outside air *in general*, at one or more sites in the house. Although they can function as fireplace air intakes, they are not designed to be installed inside the fireplace but nearby. (They're made of plastic!) Along with my idea that fireplaces are usually best fixed by increments, I tend to install one Condar at a time for an average-sized fireplace and test it before installing a second one. I usually install two for a large fireplace, i.e., 36" or wider. One of the things I like about the Condar is that it can be easily installed during construction or later.

If the Condar is installed near the floor, typically in the baseboard or right above and on either side of the fireplace, the cold current of air feeding towards the fireplace never seems noticeable. It's possible that only a small percentage of this outside air is pulled directly into the fireplace and much more likely that it first mixes with house air. My assumption had always been that Condars are opened only when the fireplace is in use. (Condars were used as air intakes on that big old house I installed the exhaust fan in, one on each side of the fireplace. It is my impression that the homeowners left them open all the time, the right decision, in my opinion, for that air-starved house.)

Although Condars are plastic, they don't look particularly obtrusive. Additionally, it's not obvious that they have anything to do with the fireplace. To my eye, they look like electric or electronic equipment of some kind.

A third strategy is introduction of outside air at the lowest point in the house, the basement floor. Because this is usually below grade, I do it as shown below. See Figure 27.

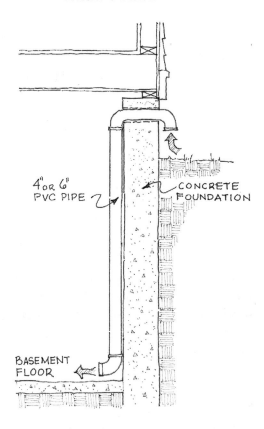

BASEMENT AIR INTAKE
FIGURE 27

4" or 6" PVC pipe or its equivalent

The opening to the outside is screened with wire mesh to prevent animals from entering. I either use the regular hardware cloth which has ½" openings or the smaller size which has ¼" openings. Regular mosquito screening would slow the air down too much.

The reason that adding air to the basement works is that significantly increasing the air pressure *in the basement* increases the air pressure *everywhere* else in the house, surprise, surprise!

Even if there doesn't seem to be any obvious way for the air to move upwards, as most basements are sealed off from the rest of the house by doors at the top of the basement stairs, it always makes a big difference. (By the same token, if we introduce air on the 1st floor, we only increase air pressure on the 1st floor and higher in the house, not in the basement below.) The difficulty is to design an air intake that will act *only* as an intake and never as an outlet, which is why I recommend introducing air onto the basement floor, the place with the lowest air pressure in the whole house. No fan is needed and no controls. I don't believe it ever quits during the heating season. But it may flow in more quickly or more slowly, according to the demand.

This intake could perhaps be closed or restricted with a cement block or some other means when you're not having a fire. (During hot weather when and if you are *cooling* the whole house, this should be closed off. If it's open, cooled air, which is naturally heavier than warm air, will probably *flow out of the house*.)

INSULATING THE CHIMNEY FLUE

I consider it a wise tactic to *insulate* the flue liner of the low chimney *as it is being built*. In conjunction with a closed top damper, this will insure that the chimney will become much warmer as heated air from inside the house migrates up the chimney. Low chimneys that I have insulated worked flawlessly.

Insulating a flue is probably much cheaper than an exhaust fan, maybe 1/3rd the cost. What must be done is to make the brick part of the chimney 1"-3" larger on each side. For insulation, I have used a slightly moistened vermiculite/Portland cement mixture. I stabilize the liners with pieces of 1/4th inch rebar at the corners of the chimney every few feet. (Normally the flue liners are stabilized by the mortar that squeezes out from the joints between the flue liners or from between the bricks. Some chimneys have mortar poured between the liners and the bricks. This is not a recommended practice because it does not give any space for thermal expansion.) I've also used Perlite or Permalite instead of vermiculite. See Figure 28.

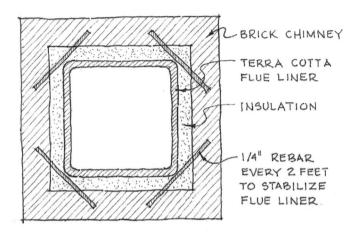

LOOKING DOWN
ON CHIMNEY

BRICK CHIMNEY

TERRA COTTA
FLUE LINER

INSULATION

1/4" REBAR
EVERY 2 FEET
TO STABILIZE
FLUE LINER.

INSULATING THE
CHIMNEY FLUE

FIGURE 28

Another non-flammable insulation, which I understand works great and probably better because it would always stay in place is mineral, rock, or ceramic wool. (I'd go with whatever wool is cheapest. We don't need a high-temperature insulation here.) Wool should be available in 1" and 2" thick batts or as a blanket roll. Insulating wool may be harder to find locally than vermiculite and the other similar materials typically found at most garden supply outlets.

While insulation may not completely solve the whole problem for every low chimney, it makes a huge difference and should insure that an exhaust fan is unnecessary.

On systemic issues in general, I think it makes sense to overkill at the outset. The most important business to handle during construction is insulating the fireplace chimney flue.

With the very unlikely result that all these steps fail to completely resolve smoking issues, glass doors or an exhaust fan can always be added.

HEALTH RISK

Not only is lack of fresh air inside our houses a problem for fireplaces, it can also negatively affect our health. Some 30 years ago, the US Consumer Products Safety Commission issued a report on the risks of tight houses, "The Inside Story, A Guide to Indoor Air Quality." (Our Government Accounting Office also issued a later report in 1991, "Indoor Air Pollution" and EPA followed with their report on the problem in 1995.) What the general public doesn't realize is that many of the construction and decorative components of a house—the paint, the carpeting, the insulation, the glue in the plywood, etc.—are all breaking down (oxidizing), albeit at a slow rate, into toxic gasses which need to be vented on a continuous basis to keep the air fit and safe to breathe. Most carpeting, for example, is sprayed with fungicides. Urea formaldehyde, used as foam insulation, is highly unstable and toxic as are the resins and glues in plywood and particleboard. The general category of one group of toxins is volatile organic compounds (VOCs), which include acetone, benzene, ethylene glycol, methylene chloride, perchloroethylene, tolyene, xylene and 1,3-butadiene. These can be in our air and in our water. For starters, they affect our breathing. Asthmatics are especially hard hit. In a way, systemic fireplace smoking problems—which are caused by lack of air and air pressure inside the house—could be called the canaries or early warning systems in our coalmine. We would do well, for our best health, to design and modify our homes so there is always plenty of fresh air inside them.

An additional health problem in our tightest houses is mold and fungus proliferation.

In the name of energy conservation we have haplessly created a new, serious environmental/health problem—toxic indoor air pollution. During the last 15 years, air-to-air heat exchangers have started to be installed in new houses, often in the basement. They are designed to preheat (or pre-cool) some of the incoming air with heat (or cool air) from the inside air that is being removed. Some designs also moisturize the incoming air in the same fashion.

This is a start at addressing this serious problem. Maybe I should revise my recommendations about Condars and we should just always leave them open.

One of the greatest ironies of this situation is that wide open chimney flues—without any kind of damper, neither at the throat or at the top, are healthier for our breathing. At least the best fireplace users will probably have outside air intakes, both Condars and basement air intakes! And fireplace users with top damper systems are still insuring lots of air changes per hour, as we will see in Chapter V.

DOWNDRAFTS

Another kind of systemic smoking problem is the downdraft, a rare problem that only occurs in a few percent of fireplaces where the air pressure at the top of the chimney momentarily exceeds the pressure at the fireplace. This is most prevalent on the slightly-pitched row house roof where there is a clutter of parapet walls, pediments, decorative turrets, other chimneys, raised skylight boxes, and air conditioner compressors. Each row house roof has its own array of features and equipment. The surprising thing to me is that a 4-foot high air conditioner compressor or parapet 25 feet away on a neighbor's roof, if wind is blowing past it in the direction of the chimney, can sometimes cause a downdraft—technically a big enough increase in air pressure to create smoking at the fireplace. The smoking is usually intermittent, because wind typically blows in gusts.

Solutions to downdraft problems are numerous and varied. Obviously, one of the fireplace myths I'd like to dispel is that *most fireplace smoking is caused by some problem at the top of the chimney.* This is untrue. Probably 95% of structural smoking is caused by design or construction mistakes *at the fireplace.* It is true that if the top of the chimney is low or if the fireplace itself is in the basement, systemic smoking is very likely. But the actual design of the chimney *termination* is only at fault (and easily correctable) if wind is the most important factor. If chimney height is poor and therefore low air pressure at the fireplace is the problem, correction is harder, as I've described.

For drawings of some of the many chimney top terminations see Figure 29.

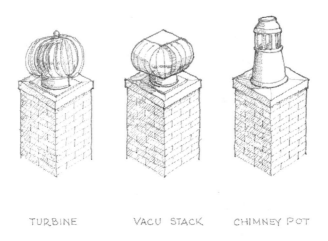

TURBINE   VACU STACK   CHIMNEY POT

CHIMNEY TOPS
FIGURE 29

Notice that many of the solutions feature a cap to deflect the wind. Sometimes the cap is not quite big enough to get the job done. I once added 3" to a 6" round cone cap all around. That extension did the trick. Another time I added 3" to each side of a top damper plate with similarly good results. See Figure 30.

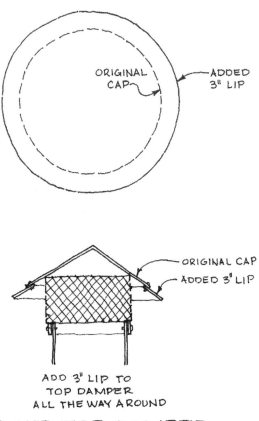

CAP AND TOP DAMPER
MADE BIGGER

FIGURE 30

Another way to tackle this kind of problem is to *restrict* the top of the chimney, as chimney pots do, as shown in Figure 29. This increases the air pressure of the exiting smoke and can often neutralize the downdraft action. Although chimney pots typically reduce the flue area around 12%, it turns out that once a chimney is warm, much greater restriction is possible, as we will see in Chapter V, with quite a wonderful result.

The obstacle causing the problem can be very near—an air conditioner compressor—or very far. I once solved a downdraft problem caused by a taller structure 300 feet away!

I think the only reason it is preferable to work on a fireplace problem at the top of the chimney—and this is not a good reason—is because it's not inside the house—you're not making a mess in the living space.

THE CAUSES AND CURES OF CHIMNEY ODORS
One fairly frequent homeowner complaint is that the fireplace smells. It can drive a homeowner nuts. The reasons for this annoying problem are fairly straightforward. Because many of our houses are so low on air, the fireplace chimney (especially an exterior one) has become an air intake, bringing along with the outside air that pungent creosote/chimney smell. (Interior chimney fireplaces never act as outside air intakes and almost never smell, even basement fireplaces.)

There are no simple cures for this systemic problem. The places to start are adding more air to the house, either with a Condar near the fireplace or installing an outside air intake into the basement. More air in the house should make the fireplace chimney behave and start drawing. Another avenue would be to install a top damper that can be closed all the way. Sometimes the problem only occurs during rainy spells. If the chimney top is moist or never dries out because the brick is faulty or because the chimney top is always in the shade, the air inside the chimney right at the top will be moist and heavier and fall down the flue and into the house, whether or not you have a top damper. Making sure the chimney top sheds rather than absorbs rainwater should make a difference. Obviously, if lots of sappy wood has been burned in a fireplace, the odors will be much stronger.

> *The ideal scenario is that there's enough air and air pressure in the house to feed the chimney so that the odors go up the chimney and not down into the house. If the homeowner never plans to use the fireplace, it can be sealed off with fiberglass insulation stuffed into the smoke chamber. The top of the chimney can also be sealed.*

UNUSUAL INSTANCES OF SYSTEMIC SMOKING

The strangest smoke problems I've ever seen are systemic, where, smoke, instead of continuing to ascend an operating, hot chimney, suddenly turns tail—takes a 180 degree turn—and comes back down into the house.

HOT AIR FURNACE RETURN LOWERING AIR PRESSURE

This case featured a forced hot air furnace *return* some 12' away from the fireplace and high on the wall. Under normal circumstances the fireplace worked great. But whenever the furnace kicked on, the fireplace would begin to smoke. It was clearly an air pressure—systemic—problem. But I hoped that strengthening the fireplace could be the answer. I made the fireplace opening smaller with that off-the-shelf 4" smoke plate I described in Chapter I. I took out a minor lip on the back wall where the damper housing was slowing down the smoke. I got a tall true grate. I even put in an outside air intake in the back wall. None of these helped at all. See Figure 31.

The solution to this kind of problem lies in adding a second furnace air return in another part of the house or, adding outside air to the furnace system. The immediate solution was turning the thermostat low enough so the furnace wouldn't come on during a fire and afterwards for several hours.

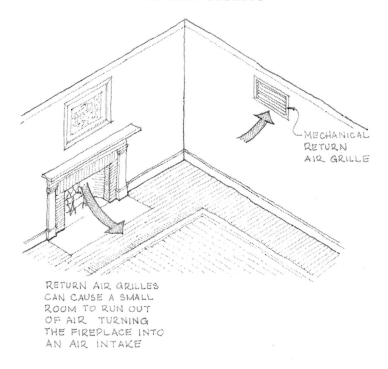

RETURN AIR GRILLES
CAN CAUSE A SMALL
ROOM TO RUN OUT
OF AIR TURNING
THE FIREPLACE INTO
AN AIR INTAKE

MECHANICAL SYSTEMS

FIGURE 31

I'm afraid that, in selected cases, lack of air pressure—i.e., a systemic problem—can trump even the strongest fireplace system, even during operation.

DAMPER USE & RUNNING OUT OF AIR

Air loss high in a house is always more serious than lower in the house simply because there's more air to lose. If lots of air is being drained from the house, systemic problems can't be far behind.

Fact: many homeowners don't use their fireplace dampers at all. They leave them open. Partly, this is because all dampers are not created equal when it comes to ease of use. Top dampers are much more user-friendly than throat dampers because their controls are in plain sight. Unless we use our fireplaces (and dampers) a lot we may never learn to manipulate the lower damper controls *kinesthetically* (by feel), almost a necessity because otherwise we can't see what we're doing without getting down on our knees with a flashlight in hand.

On one job, I was asked to install dampers for 3 fireplaces, all of which were in the same chimneystack. I ended up installing two regular dampers on the 1st and 2nd floor fireplaces and a more user-friendly top damper, which I imagined the lady of the house and its owner would be more likely to close, on the 3rd. I carefully showed her how they operated—I made her actually open and close them—and advised closing them when their fireplaces weren't in use.

About 6 months later, I got a frantic call in the middle of an early spring day. She had lit a nice big fire in the 2nd floor fireplace, which had burned fine for about an hour and then began to smoke like crazy.

When I arrived the next day, I was surprised that the room with the first floor fireplace smelled of creosote. I checked inside and saw that its damper was open. I then went to the 2nd floor. That room still smelled strongly not of creosote but of smoke. Its damper was still open. I then went to the 3rd floor, the top of the house. Its damper was also open but the room did not smell of anything. I asked the owner if she had opened the 1st and 3rd floor dampers after the smoking incident to get the smoke out. She said no, she'd just opened windows. She had not touched the dampers.

What must have happened is that the operating 2nd *and* dormant 3rd floor fireplaces were drawing so much house air that eventually the *house simply ran out of air*, i.e., reduced the interior air pressure below that of the outside at the top of the chimney. The reason the room with the 1st floor fireplace smelled of creosote is that its flue was acting as the primary air intake to displace the air being lost up the 2nd and 3rd floor fireplace chimneys. Eventually, however, it couldn't keep up.

What I found most interesting is that it was the hot and drawing 2nd floor fireplace flue that became the path of least resistance for air to enter the house, not the cooler 3rd floor fireplace flue. Obviously, it was a question of air pressure—much less on the 2nd than on the 3rd floor.

Although most homeowners say they want dampers, they don't necessarily use them. The owner of this house had refused to use her fireplaces until I'd installed dampers. (She insisted on calling them "flues" no matter how many times I corrected her.) But once the dampers were installed, she used them but once: she opened them. I don't think she ever closed them. This was not serious on the 1st floor but on the 3rd, where there's the most air and air pressure, it really was serious because the house was constantly being drained of air. It was also serious on the 2nd floor, but less so. I'm amazed she didn't have problems right away. I think a strong case can be made for installing glass doors on upper floor fireplaces, especially top floor fireplaces. While it's not possible to close a regular damper all the way right at the end of a fire, *it's obvious and easy to close glass doors.* The practice would guarantee much higher air pressure throughout the house below. It would save lots and lots on heating bills and, of course, 1st floor (and 2nd floor!) fireplaces would work much more reliably.

I should mention here another job I had, at a very big trophy mansion, which happened to have a fireplace in the third floor hallway at the top of an impressive open stairwell. I was supposed to be sweeping the fireplaces on the 1st and 2nd floors, not this fireplace, which, I was told, was never used and didn't even need to be inspected. The homeowner's heating contractor was there and, in chatting with him, I learned that the owner had been harassing him for months about how high his heating bills were. The contractor had evidently tried everything he could think of, to no avail. Well, I checked this 3rd floor fireplace and I discovered that it had no damper at all and that its smoke chamber and flue were completely coated with more than a 2" blanket of packed house dust, obviously an accumulation over the 80-year life of the house, literally tens of thousands of dollars of heating fuel having been thrown away. I plugged it with fiberglass insulation and, the homeowner told me later, cut his monthly heating bill literally in half.

This is another reason to install glass doors on fireplaces in the upper floors of a house.

THE TWO-FIREPLACE PROBLEM: SMOKE CROSSOVER

Another kind of systemic smoking problem, mercifully rare, which architects are in a position to prevent, can occur when there are two or more fireplaces on different floors, venting into the same multi-flued chimney. The problem: when you use the upper fireplace, some smoke comes out of the lower fireplace, even though the damper for the lower fireplace is closed. (Few fireplace throat dampers close 100%.) The most usual configuration for this problem is an operating 1st floor fireplace and a dormant basement fireplace. I've never seen it with an operating 2nd floor fireplace and a dormant 1st floor one but I'm sure it has happened.

Although it seems logical, and some homeowners won't hear otherwise, that the smoke is being drawn from the *very top* of the chimney, I believe that is only rarely the case. The problem, called crossover, is happening lower down, usually at more than one site, from the working flue to the dormant flue, often starting as low as the firebox itself.

Two conditions must exist for crossover to happen. The first, which applies to both kinds of crossover, is that the lower fireplace chimney must *already* (when there is no fire) be acting as an outside air intake, i.e., air must be streaming down the flue into the basement.

The second condition, which applies to the more likely *internal crossover*, is that there must exist one or more passageways or breaches between the two flues. Because of the lower air pressure in the flue drawing in the outside air, some of the smoke is pulled *sideways* from the active flue into the other flue. See Figure 32.

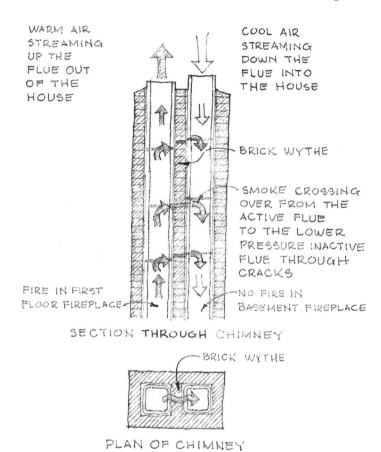

WARM AIR STREAMING UP THE FLUE OUT OF THE HOUSE

COOL AIR STREAMING DOWN THE FLUE INTO THE HOUSE

BRICK WYTHE

SMOKE CROSSING OVER FROM THE ACTIVE FLUE TO THE LOWER PRESSURE INACTIVE FLUE THROUGH CRACKS

FIRE IN FIRST FLOOR FIREPLACE

NO FIRE IN BASEMENT FIREPLACE

SECTION THROUGH CHIMNEY

BRICK WYTHE

PLAN OF CHIMNEY

TWO FIREPLACE PROBLEM
FIGURE 32

In addition to the relatively tight house, the other villain in this tale is the sloppy work of the chimney builder. First, he should have been sawing flue liners where necessary to make the best possible fits, angling the cuts where the flue turns, and mortaring between them very carefully so they couldn't leak. Even more importantly, he should have been making the row of bricks *between* the flues—called *the wythe*—absolutely air-tight, laying those bricks with extra care. I understand that these wythes were recently made code requirements in some jurisdictions. (Some chimneys were built without wythes.) When I have built multi-flued chimneys, I not only make the wythe bricks airtight, I also parge the wythe on both sides, further insuring that smoke can't be drawn laterally from flue to flue.

Where architects can make a big difference is explaining to the chimney builder that the flues must be completely isolated from each other. It wouldn't hurt to actually climb up on the scaffold and check the work. While the builders may think you're crazy, it's important to nip this problem in the bud during the construction phase. It's very expensive to repair after-the-fact.

(For some bricklayers, taking care with brickwork that will never be visible to the public is not something they see a point in doing.)

One fix that *always makes these crossovers worse* is to install a top damper on the offending flue. (If the smoke were crossing over at the tops of the chimneys, a closed top damper would solve it.) What typically happens with a top damper is that even *more* smoke is now drawn from within the working flue into the dormant flue. And, remember, what's driving this whole process is the low air pressure in the basement.

The *technical* fix to this systemic problem is to add lots and lots of air on a continuous basis to the basement. Another fix is to seal off the lower fireplace by packing fiberglass in the throat. I have found that rebuilding the smoke chamber of the upper fireplace where necessary and then carefully parging it with mortar to make it absolutely airtight solves about half of these crossovers. There are also other fixes, none of them cheap. I have first rebuilt the working smoke chamber and then begun mortaring the joints between the flue liners by cutting into the chimney at every joint and working from *inside* the liners. I would test the fireplace after doing each joint. The smoking always decreased each time but never quit completely until I had done *all the joints*. Others have knocked out the old terra cotta liners and installed a continuous stainless steel sleeve. You're talking thousands of dollars with either fix. Merely sleeving the leaking fireplace flue liner with a stainless steel liner will significantly diminish its size and create a ratio smoke problem, so cannot stand alone as a real fix. Incidentally, I have never seen smoke crossover when the entire chimney was interior and therefore *warm*.

A most sobering moments for me was trying to solve this problem by cutting into, from the outside, the chimney flue of the unused (but smoking!) lower fireplace and sealing up the inside of the flue completely with fiberglass and a 3-inch layer of mortar. It didn't work. This low air pressure dynamic was so powerful that smoke continued to be sucked down into the basement but now between the brick and the outside of the sealed flue liner.

Another solution if there are 2 fireplaces is to first light the lower fireplace (which may not be that easy or convenient) *before* lighting the fireplace above. And then keep *both* fireplaces going.

The first chapter was my attempt to explain the dynamics of fireplaces and chimneys in the simplest way possible, especially to homeowners interested in diagnosing and solving many of their smoking problems on their own. But it is also a useful introduction for architects to be reminded of how fireplaces and chimneys actually work and for them to better fulfill their roles as fireplace magicians behind the curtain. My second chapter highlighted a fireplace feature that is widely neglected in US today, the degree of splay of a fireplace's sidewalls. In this chapter, the third, I've been outlining the roots of systemic smoke problems and building on this understanding to insure better fireplace and chimney design and construction.

FIREPLACE RULES FOR ARCHITECTS

Fireplaces should be designed and built according to certain rules. If they are not, they will probably smoke. Some of the rules can be found in the architect's Bible, Architectural Graphic Standards. One rule that architects pay the most attention to is the recommended ratio between the fireplace opening and a cross section of the flue. For fireplaces with short chimneys, 10'-16', the ratio should 8 to 1. For fireplaces with medium tall chimneys, 16'-28', it should be 10 to 1, and with taller chimneys, 12 to 1. As we shall see, however, there are many conditions that can change these ratios in a big way, sometimes to the good.

My beef with Architectural Graphic Standards is that it conveys vital information *mainly* with its drawings despite widespread deviations in practice. For instance, it is never indicated that a lip on the back wall made by the throat damper housing can cause smoking even though some 20% of fireplaces are built this way today. Another rule, also only *shown* and not verbally described, is the placement of the damper, which should be 8" above the top of the fireplace opening and *all the way* forward against the inside of the chimneybreast.

Most serious is that Graphic Standards never alerts the architect to the problem of fireplaces with low chimneys.

My structural rules are listed below. Perhaps the most interesting point about this list is that you may only need 4 of the 5 to have a more or less workable fireplace. Unfortunately, but understandably, fireplace structural mistakes usually come in clusters.

Rule 1: *No ledges* should be on the back and sides where the firebox meets the damper housing. *One reason this mistake is made is because the fireplace builder does not want to go to the trouble of sawing notches in the back wall bricks where they meet*

the damper housing. Instead, he just lays them up behind the 1.5"
damper housing frame.

Rule 2: Make sure the splay or angle of the sidewalls is sufficient, a subject I discussed in Chapter II. *To insure that the fireplace builder builds the firebox with sufficient splay, the architect should draw, at the outset, the fireplace's correct trapezoidal shape on the hearth, something fireplace builders often do on their own, using the damper housing as their template. Architects should use the digital angle meter to demonstrate the angle they're proposing, preferably 115. But don't increase the splay so much that the back wall is less than 20" wide.*

Rule 3: If the fireplace opening is taller than 30 inches, increase the splay 2 degrees for every inch higher than 30". *Not mentioned in Architectural Graphic Standards.*

Rule 4: Make every attempt to install the damper as far forward as possible. This is easier done with the better damper designs.

Rule 5: Fireplace opening and flue size must be in *correct ratio.* Some architects draw up the plans with the *exact interior dimensions* of the firebox even though *many fireplace builders tend to ignore specific directions because they assume that they know better and that it doesn't really make much difference anyway. Incidentally, I have seen drawings where architects pass the buck and intentionally leave the area of the firebox completely blank, as if only the fireplace mechanic knew what the correct geometry should be.*

The major driver of systemic smoke problems is always lack of air and air pressure inside the house at the fireplace. Chimneys are never drawing smoke only, as I've pointed out, but a *combination of smoke and house air.* If there is no fire in the fireplace and the damper is open or even just leaking a little, it will still be drawing air out of the house, at least in an ideal world.

The three most important rules to prevent *systemic* smoking are:

Rule 1: If a fireplace chimney is *lower* than other chimneys on the house or than the tallest part of the house, it's important to inform clients that there will be a smoking problem and to insist *that the flue of this low chimney, which is almost always exterior, be insulated.* Additionally, they should be told that top dampers and/or glass doors may also be required. *Low chimneys work far better if they are insulated.*

Rule 2: A basement fireplace should have a raised hearth, both inside the firebox and the outer hearth being the same height. Fourteen to 16 inches should do the job. Basements typically have the least amount of air in the whole house and, near the basement floor, the least amount of all. The whole house must have more air if a basement fireplace is to draw properly. *It's counter-intuitive to the regular fireplace builder that basement fireplaces should be so different from fireplaces located elsewhere in the house. Top dampers and/or glass doors may also be required.*

Rule 3: Attention must be given to supplying adequate amounts of outside air to a new or fully renovated house, which is probably very tight with improved windows and more insulation. *No fireplace will work correctly without adequate air pressure in the house.* A powerful kitchen exhaust fan can cripple a perfectly designed fireplace. A simple option: warn homeowners to crack a window in the kitchen before they turn on the exhaust fan. Consider installing one or two Condar units in the kitchen, near floor level. *Only heating engineers are trained to think about air and some are better trained in this than others. Architects must discuss their concerns (and solutions) with their heating engineers and, if possible, overkill on bringing outside air into the house system.*

Architectural Graphic Standards never mentions Condar outside air intakes, which, in my experience, work far better than the air intakes inside the firebox.

I hereby challenge architects to take responsibility for structural and, even more importantly, systemic smoke problems. Designing houses that have lots of healthy fresh air should also be an architect's duty. If not the architect, who else?

Summary

How to design low chimneys that work. The exhaust fan as a default solution. Benefits of insulating low exterior chimneys. Ceramic wool batts, if available, are probably the best insulation. Importance of outside air for smoke-free fireplace operation. Smoking sometimes caused by wind. How to solve chimney odors. Serious health risks of too tight houses. Smoking caused by running out of air.

CHAPTER IV

MORE SMOKING SOLUTIONS

CONTENTS

Aluminum foil test—Perfect Fireplace—Significance of when a fireplace starts to smoke—Smoking Checklist—Best Designed Fireplaces—Correct Screening—Process of Elimination—Permanent Smoke Plates—Raising Inner Hearth—Making Whole Fireboxes Smaller—New Damper Controls—Adding to Chimney Height—Smoke Chambers—Why Fireplaces Need Stability—More Fireplace Myths Dispelled

ALUMINUM FOIL SMOKE TEST

Let's assume you know a fireplace smokes but you don't know exactly how much. (You may also not know if the smoking is structural or systemic.) By blocking off the top of the fireplace opening with aluminum foil held in place by masking tape, you make the fireplace small enough so that, during a small test fire, it works without smoking. Then, little by little, you roll the foil up, gradually enlarging the fireplace so you can determine the point at which it starts smoking. See Figure 33.

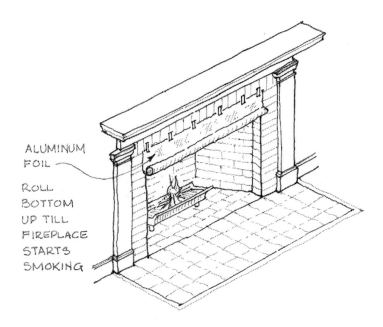

ALUMINUM
FOIL

ROLL
BOTTOM
UP TILL
FIREPLACE
STARTS
SMOKING

ALUMINUM FOIL TEST

FIGURE 33

This test also tells you whether the smoking is structural or systemic. If, right from the start before starting to roll up the aluminum foil, the smoking problem is solved, you know beyond a shadow of a doubt that the smoking is structural, i.e., caused by defects in the design and/or construction of the fireplace. In other words, the fireplace is not smoking because of lack of air in the house. After you've rolled the foil up enough so that fireplace begins to smoke shows you another vital piece of information: the depth of the foil still remaining is the *minimum size* of the smoke plate/guard needed to correct the smoke problem.

While I used the test more before my discovery of splay, I still find occasions where this test provides information that is invaluable to a smoke plate solution. It adds precise quantification to my diagnosis.

For smoking problems, which, I suspect, to be relatively minor, I start with foil hanging down 4"-6". For worse ones or, if I have no idea how serious the smoking might be, I start with 6"-8". I then build a very small fire, mainly with kindling—medium dry twigs will do, we want some smoke—and observe whether the foil at this size has stopped the smoking. Sometimes you can see it spilling out. But I also sniff along the edge of the foil because you can always *smell smoke* well before you can see it. If you smell a hint of smoke or even of heat, the fireplace is smoking. Over the years I have used many different tools, besides my eyes and my nose, to detect smoke leaking out, including a flashlight, a stick of lighted incense or even just a match, lit or just blown out and smoking. The most versatile tool, I've decided, is the gas grill igniter. Just watch how its flame behaves as you hold it at the very top of the fireplace opening (or, in this case) the lower lip of the aluminum foil. If the fireplace is operating correctly, air from the house (and the flame from the igniter) will always be move *into the fireplace, without fail.*

As I'm gradually rolling the aluminum foil up about ½" at a time, I've noticed that the test signals right away if it's starting to smoke with the new dimension or with the next. Air flowing (or incense smoke or the igniter flame) under the lip of the foil will stutter step, i.e., it almost starts to smoke (or reverse) and then pulls the smoke back in. I continue to feed the little fire I started as I roll the foil up. Remember that the size of the test fire is not a factor. A small test fire will tell you just as much as a big test fire. The beauty of this test is that you don't have to commit to a big fire to get extremely useful information. Even a little smoke leaking out of a fireplace is rarely caused by the volume of normal, regular smoke or hot gasses but, surprisingly, because of other factors. When I've found the optimal size of fireplace opening where it's not smoking but a bigger size starts it smoking—the cusp or pivot point—I can then proceed, either with a factory-made plate or a specially-fabricated smoke plate or its equivalent in new brickwork faced with stone or tile.

If the fireplace chimney is on the outside of the house —an exterior fireplace system and therefore colder—you should probably do this test more than once when the chimney is at its coldest. Also, remember that a large test fire can confound the issue by adding lots of heat. You need to know how the chimney system performs dead cold, right at the beginning of a fire.

When sizing a smoke plate or its masonry equivalent, I tend to add up to a half an inch to the pivot point, i.e., where it starts to smoke. For example, if it started to smoke at 4" below the top of the fireplace opening, I'd make the smoke plate (or its equivalent) more than 4" up to 4.5".

For the record, Benjamin Franklin writes about testing fireplace-opening-size using lumber to temporarily reduce the size of the fireplace opening. In his time and earlier, the chimney cloth, what could be called an adjustable fireplace curtain, may have done a similar job for working fireplaces. The cloth would be lowered as you were starting the fire and then rolled up once the chimney was hot and drawing well. Paintings of the time, which feature fireplaces with chimney cloths draped at-the-ready right below the mantel, are of large kitchen fireplaces. Cooking is usually in progress.

The chimney cloth, if long enough, may also have been useful during sweeping by trapping the falling soot inside the fireplace.

Technically, what a smoke plate (or chimney cloth) does is to change *the ratio* between the fireplace opening and the size of the flue, making the fireplace opening small enough so the unheated chimney can draw or handle all the smoke. I explain more about these ratios in Chapter V.

I got the idea for the aluminum foil test from an old Charles Dickens movie where, to start a fireplace chimney drawing, an old man lights the fire, holds a folded out newspaper over the upper portion of the fireplace opening, and then, when the chimney starts to draw, removes the newspaper. I've tried it and the pesky fireplace often starts drawing in seconds, well before the newspaper catches fire! This is still an elegant, inexpensive trick for an on-the-cusp fireplace although most modern American fireplaces are typically wider than our longest newspapers. A correctly-sized piece of cardboard or a piece of light plywood could be pressed into service momentarily every time you start a fire if you don't like the look (or cost) of a smoke plate. (A larger smoke guard or plate, covering the whole fireplace opening except for a ½" slit at the bottom, could even do what we saw glass doors do in Chapter I to correct a serious smoke problem, that is close off the opening until the chimney can heat up and begin to draw.)

To repeat, the reason to do the aluminum foil test is to find out *how much smaller* the fireplace needs to be for the fireplace to work without smoking—right from the start. Sometimes you only need an inch or two of foil or smoke plate, sometimes so much that more ambitious strategies, like glass doors or major reconstruction, are called for.

While lowering the top of the fireplace is the most popular tactic for solving a smoke problem, actually raising the hearth can also be effective, which I discuss in a moment.

(I take the precaution of always having aluminum foil and masking tape available when familiarizing myself with a fireplace. It's a foolproof fallback position if a full-blown fire suddenly starts smoking—a rare but not unheard of event— even though you thought you'd solved the problem. Trying to put out a big fire in a fireplace is never easy and can be dangerous. If you can control the smoke with the foil, best to let it burn out. When testing a fireplace you just repaired is another moment you may need the help of foil and masking tape, if things happen to go awry.)

I would like to point out that everyone involved with fireplace smoking would do well to utilize the aluminum foil test. Often, when I've examined smoking fireplaces that others had tried to fix, I've noticed that the smoking problem had not been accurately diagnosed in the first place. (And, of course, the test can also be used to reveal if whatever fix that had been done was successful.)

But don't expect a homeowner to perform this test! While it may seem very straightforward to someone in the fireplace business, I've never been able to persuade a homeowner to try it, even after giving detailed instructions.

THE PERFECT FIREPLACE

Hand in hand with the aluminum foil test, I came to the realization that one can easily achieve *the perfect fireplace*, i.e., one that never smokes. What the aluminum foil test did was confirm the patterns I'd observed in fireplaces that smoke and ones that didn't.

A perfect fireplace, for example, has the correct ratio, 1 to 10 or, for taller chimneys, 1 to 12 or, for really tall chimneys, it turns out, much more. Interior or insulated chimneys can have bigger ratios.

Another important feature of the perfect fireplace is the location of the throat damper. Dampers at the back of the firebox never work well until the chimney is really hot. All the way forward always works much, much better.

If the damper is the same height as the fireplace opening, start-up is often shaky. By far the best position was all the way forward and at least 4.5" above the fireplace opening and, for a really strong fireplace, 8" or 9".

Regarding the splay of the sidewalls, I blindly accepted that 110 degrees must be the correct angle, the rear housing angle on the throat dampers available to me at that time. See Figure 9 in Chapter II. But, for some reason, I never even considered for almost 20 years that *increasing this angle would or could change fireplace performance.* Boy, do I feel stupid that I missed this for so many years!

Notice that all these specifications I listed above affect structural smoking, not systemic.

WHEN SMOKING STARTS IS AN IMPORTANT CLUE

Exactly *when a fireplace smokes or starts smoking* is often a crucial piece of information. If it only occurs at the beginning of the fire and then corrects itself within less than a minute, it is likely a minor ratio error, a minor lip on the back wall, a damper too low or sidewall splay a little less than 110 degrees—or some combination of these minor flaws. All these are structural problems. Remember this is a dynamic situation, especially at the beginning of a fire. Small changes in heat and air supply can affect performance. The key thing to remember is if a reasonable quantity of smoke and hot gasses are able to make it up the chimney, the chimney will warm up and start drawing strongly enough to solve the problem. (Even if this only takes a couple of minutes, you may still want to fix it. Smoking even on a small, brief scale can become annoying. Smoke odors can linger.)

If the smoking is more than a few percent and the smoke is leaking out everywhere—not only at the top of the fireplace opening—it's almost certainly a systemic problem, well, probably *also* a systemic problem, the lack-of-air-in-the-house problem, which I discussed in Chapter III. If the smoking occurs intermittently, it's almost certainly a wind-created downdraft. If the fireplace works fine for an hour or so and then starts smoking, it's probably that the room with the fireplace or the house itself is running low on air. What will happen is that the fireplace will smoke briefly because of outside air coming *down* the chimney and then, when the air pressure in the house is somewhat restored, start working again for a period of time. This cycle is usually reinforced by people opening windows to get the smoke out. If it seems *unpredictable*, make sure it's not caused by a kitchen or bathroom exhaust fan or a hot air furnace starting up.

Always check the firewood. Bad wood, which creates lots of smoke along with steam, while rarely the only cause of smoking, muddies your analysis. In some instances, upgrading the firewood—burning perfectly seasoned wood with a tall, true grate—can reduce a smoke problem so much that you're inclined to just live with it. (I've had customers brag that they liked the smell of a *little* wood smoke.)

If a first floor fireplace that was used successfully in the past but hasn't been used for some years, is then fired up and smokes badly right from the get-go, it could be a squirrel's nest, especially if the chimney is unscreened at the top. While squirrels' nests are usually built right at the chimney top, usually when there is shelter from the rain and snow, these nests almost always slump down too far to be usable. (Squirrels are very determined workers but terrible engineers.) They are the only animals that make this kind of nest, at least in the United States. Raccoons, for instance, don't build nests. They just move in! Raccoons are the only animals I know of that can (and will) negotiate the inside of a vertical tube like a chimney. They then set up home on a fireplace smoke shelf, have babies, and raise them there. (More on raccoons in Chapter VIII.)

In some ways squirrels are a bigger problem than raccoons. If they happen to fall down a chimney flue and there is access to the inside of the house through an open fireplace damper, they can and will cause lots of damage. In my experience, raccoons rarely cause any damage even if they get into the house. They seem to intuitively know the rules of good clean living.

Or the chimney blockage could be man-made inadvertently or on purpose. Chimney lore has it that, in the good old days, the chimney builder would block the flue with a pane of glass, usually at the top of the chimney. He'd only break the glass after he'd been paid. But anyone looking up the chimney flue from the inside would think it was free and clear.

I remember one job I did where it looked like a brick was partly bridging the flue liner about half way up the chimney, possibly, I thought, a less subtle version of the pane-of-glass tactic. I could still see light, just not as much as I should have. I described the problem to the homeowner, saying I could cut into the chimney from the next-door row house, which had been gutted for renovation, and not make a mess in his house. I returned on Sunday when the workmen weren't there, cut in, removed the brick, and repaired the hole I'd made. The family was not home so I telephoned later and instructed them to try it in a couple of days after the mortar had cured. They did and it worked fine. But their young children were quite upset. They ran to the kitchen and reported that there was something wrong with the fireplace. "No smoke's coming out!" They had never experienced a fireplace that didn't smoke. They obviously thought that was the point.

Sometimes a problem is so easily solved, it's hardly a job at all. In one such case the smoking never quit but was clearly structural because smoke was only leaking out along the top of the fireplace opening. I found a number of possible explanations. The damper was too low, only about 3 inches above the fireplace opening, the damper a little too far back. The splay of the sidewalls was slightly less than 110. The wood was not great. The basement seemed low on air, which, I've found, can affect how well a 1st floor fireplace draws. On the last step of my investigation, which was to use my ladder to examine the chimney top, I discovered the cause. The chimney cap had slumped a couple of inches, which ended up slightly restricting the smoke as it tried to exit the chimney. Finally, I took the last step of my investigation, which was to put my ladder up to the chimney top. What I discovered turned out to be the cause. A cheap factory-made chimney cap— all of these caps, inexpensive aluminum ones and fancy stainless steel ones, are ugly in my opinion but sometimes necessary— I raised the cap and tightened the strap around the top of the flue liner, which was supposed to keep the cap at the right height. I also caulked the strap in place. This idiotically simple fix was successful. I didn't have to do anything else. I estimate that 1/3 of my jobs were on this level: the problem was real but the fix very obvious and low-cost. (All factory-made chimney caps, by the way, even the expensive stainless caps, are, in my opinion, obtrusive and ugly. If possible, I prefer masonry solutions or the less obtrusive homemade caps, which I describe in a few pages.)

SMOKING CHECKLIST

As I'm looking at a smoking fireplace I know has *structural* smoking problems, I mentally go through a list of possible causes, many of which I have already described and some I will get to momentarily.

- Incorrect ratio between fireplace opening and the inside of the flue
- Lack of adequate sidewall splay
- Damper housing ledge at the top of the back wall of the firebox or on each side
- Damper set too low or too far back
- Damper plate/door not opening all the way
- Ledge right above damper opening
- Chimney flue blocked by faulty screening, a creosote-encrusted screen, or a squirrel's nest.

Note that 5 of the 7 causes are related to the throat damper. It is no accident that the best-designed fireplaces I have ever seen had no throat damper at all. (Also note that all of these flaws, with the exception of the bad screen and squirrel's nest, could conceivably be solved just by increasing the splay.)

Although the homeowner wrongly believes that the reason his fireplace smokes must be *his fault, of his own doing*, i.e., he didn't pay attention at Boy Scouts, he is always wrong, as this list shows.

A smoking fireplace is not a user problem. It's a builder problem. Incidentally, it's also not that your chimney needs sweeping.

> *BEST-DESIGNED FIREPLACES I'VE EVER SEEN*
>
> *The fireplaces I have in mind are located near a part of Washington, DC called Carter Barron. They were obviously built by the same hand. The splay of their sidewalls is between 115 and 120 degrees. The back wall is angled forward starting about 16" high in the firebox. The opening to the smoke chamber ranges from 2.5" to 3" and is always 10" or more above the top of the fireplace opening. It is all the way to the front. To my eye, it looked like a Rumford cousin could have built them.*
>
> *Even though throat dampers were available when these fireplaces were built, none have them. I'm pretty certain these were built sometime between 1910 and 1930. Usable fireplace dampers became available in the United States starting in the 1890's.*
>
> *It is my impression that individual fireplace builders have made technical discoveries/breakthroughs on their own for literally hundreds of years but virtually none of these discoveries have ever been written down. I consider Rumford, who rebuilt 100's of fireplaces AND wrote about what he discovered, the exception to this rule. He was primarily a scientist with a very practical bent. More on Rumford in Chapter IX.*

LEDGE REMOVAL

The other major fireplace fix besides new splay that requires working with bricks and mortar inside the fireplace is the *removal* or *smoothing out* of ledges formed by the incorrect installation of throat dampers. The most serious is when the top brick is not notched around the damper housing at the top of the back wall. Because it's almost always impossible to slide or move the damper housing, usually held in place by brickwork at its front, what must be done is to take down two or three courses of the back wall and relay them, with more forward pitch, sawing notches in the top brick. The way I usually do this is to relay the top 7" to 8" with "sailor" brick, i.e., brick laid with the 4.5" face angling into the room. I notch/saw the ends to fit around the damper housing lip. These brick usually end up more pitched than the rest of the back wall. See Figure 34.

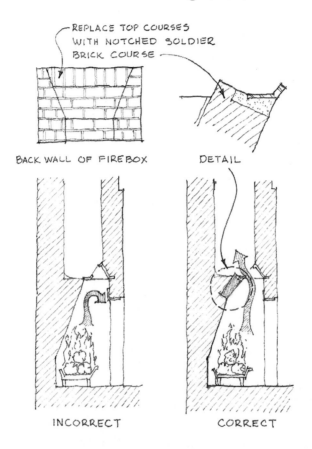

BACK LEDGE REMOVAL
FIGURE 34

In a properly functioning fireplace, the back wall is the chief pathway for flames, smoke, and hot gasses to exit the firebox. Even the typical 1.5" damper housing ledge is large enough to obstruct this pathway and cause smoking, especially at the beginning of a fire before the chimney is hot and drawing hard. It is also the case that even If this exposed part of the housing does not, for some reason, cause smoking, it will eventually warp, buckle and break with long hot fires. For this reason, it's important to rebuild the top of the back wall to protect this part of the damper housing. When this piece is gone, there's no simple, affordable way to repair or rebuild the damper. This is a good example of extremely sloppy fireplace construction ending badly.

Ledges are sometimes found at the top of the sidewalls of the fireplace if the damper is undersized or if the splay of the sidewalls is less than the 110 degrees of the damper housing. These sidewall ledges are much less serious than back wall ledges if under 2". I have found that as long as they are *smoothed out*, i.e., made gradual and less abrupt with built-up layers of mortar, they don't cause any smoking. (It's always doubly satisfying to take out or greatly reduce these side ledges as part of increasing the angle of the sidewalls with new splay.)

I have unsuccessfully tried a similar smoothing-out tactic on the back wall ledge. It worked initially but then always fell off after a few fires. There is much more heat at the back of a fireplace than on the sides and only brick reconstruction works.

If a customer has both inadequate splay and a bad ledge on the back wall, I tend to correct the ledge first. Sometimes, if there is more than one problem with the fireplace, i.e., inadequate splay, damper housing ledge on back wall, non-heat resistant mortar, etc., I press to redo the whole firebox.

For many years, I assumed that ledges only mattered on the sides and the back, not on the front. Although nowhere near as serious, front ledges, if more than 2", can also be a contributing cause to fireplaces smoking. (Obviously if you have the damper housing set against the inside front of the chimney breast, there will only be a lip of about ½", which never seems to create a problem.) See Figure 35.

INCORRECT CORRECT

FRONT LEDGE REMOVAL

FIGURE 35

Judgment is often required to determine the worst problem, the ledge or poor splay. Then the expense of the repair(s) must be considered. It's crucial to include the expense of the cure in your plan.

CORRECT SCREENING

Faulty screening at the top of a chimney must be considered as a serious if infrequent problem. The best screening is made from 2" X 2" hardware cloth, sometimes called rat wire. The holes are a full half-inch square. The wire is skinny, less than the diameter of the lead in an automatic pencil. I describe screen fabrication details in a moment.

It's important that any screen be raised 4" to 6" above the top of the flue liner. This means there is a larger area of screening for the smoke to escape through. If a screen is laid *flat* on the top of the flue liner, it is possible that creosote will build up even on skinny wires and start obstructing or slowing the smoke down. If the wire is thick or the holes less than ½", it's even more likely to cause obstruction. Figure 36.

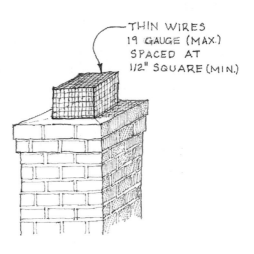

THIN WIRES
19 GAUGE (MAX.)
SPACED AT
1/2" SQUARE (MIN.)

CORRECT RAISED SCREEN
FIGURE 36

If rain is prevented from washing the screen clean, this can end up causing smoking. On one job I had, a factory-made rain cap/screen with large holes and thick wire became completely blocked with creosote. The chimney had recently been cleaned *from the fireplace*, the usual practice, but the sweep never checked the rain cap.

Another time, the correct wire with ½" openings was laid flat over the top of the chimney, *underneath* a factory-made rain cap, which had a manufactured screen of its own. Again, rain couldn't keep the screen clean and the fireplace began to smoke. Another time, a raised screen had ¼" openings instead of the ½" openings. The fireplace would work fine for 3 or 4 fires at the beginning of each season and then begin to smoke. The following year, after rain had done its job, the fireplace would work again for a few fires.

For fabrication details of a correct screen, see Figure 37.

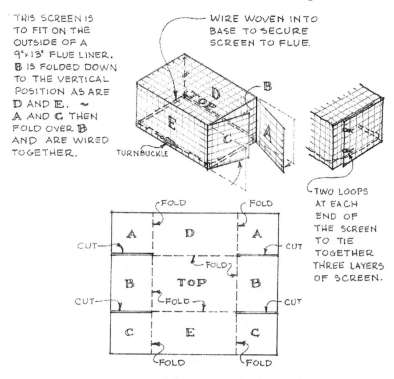

THIS SCREEN IS TO FIT ON THE OUTSIDE OF A 9"x13" FLUE LINER. B IS FOLDED DOWN TO THE VERTICAL POSITION AS ARE D AND E. A AND C THEN FOLD OVER B AND ARE WIRED TOGETHER.

WIRE WOVEN INTO BASE TO SECURE SCREEN TO FLUE.

TURNBUCKLE

TWO LOOPS AT EACH END OF THE SCREEN TO TIE TOGETHER THREE LAYERS OF SCREEN.

HANDMADE SCREEN
FIGURE 37

Notice that the screen fits *outside* the flue liner. Although I prefer the use of an aluminum turnbuckle—a steel turnbuckle will rust—as the method for securing the screen with 12-gauge galvanized wire, the wire alone, drawn tightly, and then crimped for tightening at several locations works almost as well.

If there is no flue liner sticking up to attach the screen to, you cement it in place, usually by first bending the bottom of the screen out at 90 degrees and then adding a layer of concrete to that lip.

I prefer screens I make myself because I find the factory-made screen/cap combinations very obtrusive. If possible, I like keeping chimneys as much masonry as possible.

An important point about brick and masonry in general is that they are hygroscopic, which means they absorb and release water vapor according to ambient temperature and humidity. So under normal circumstances, chimneys don't really need rain caps. There is sufficient evaporation of moisture to prevent water from reaching the lower part of the flue. But, if the whole becomes water-logged, say on a one-story house, a factory-made chimney cap really does make sense. But if the chimney is 20' high but still moist, a 1/16" thick galvanized metal plate can be attached to the top of the screen whose fabrication I just described. To attach the plate, typically oversized by 1" to 2" on each side, I drill 4 holes in the plate and then attach it to the screen with 1-inch or shorter 1/8th" stove bolts and fender washers above the plate and underneath the screening, one bolt near each corner. The idea is not to try to stop all rain from entering the chimney. It's to cut the amount by 75 to 80%. The other good feature with this design rain cap is that most of the screen on the 4 sides is kept clean by driving rain. Factory-made caps, as I mentioned above, block the rain so well that it is kept from reaching the screen at all and cleaning it.

The reason I like to screen chimneys venting gas boilers and furnaces is to prevent leaves from falling down the flue but also to keep out the occasional squirrel or bird who falls in by mistake.

I don't believe squirrels or birds ever go down a flue on purpose. I remember discovering two desiccated squirrel corpses in close embrace on a smoke shelf. I assume they were playing and fell down the chimney. Or maybe one fell and the other went down to help. Lack of water would have killed them before lack of food.

Fireplace flues should always be screened, especially unused ones, to keep out raccoons. I've noticed that fireplace use in many households is sporadic. Years may go by when there is little use and then, suddenly, the fireplace, if it once worked well, starts to be used again.

For the record, animals do not like the smell of a chimney that is used (or has been recently used) for venting smoke/gasses from burning wood, coal or oil and will shun it. If a chimney smells a little bad or strong to us, it smells truly horrible to an animal. (Hint: it can smell plenty bad to even the most hardened chimney sweep if lots of unseasoned wood has been burned!) Animals also don't like chimneys that are warm, which is the reason they tend to stay away from even unscreened chimneys where natural gas is the fuel for heating domestic hot water all year long and, during the winter, for space heating as well. There is no noticeable odor because natural gas burns so cleanly, but the high temperatures are intolerable to animals. The exception is on a very cold day when some birds will actually sit or stand on top of a screen serving a chimney for a natural gas heater. A young, long-haired TV antenna installer gave me a different explanation, as we stood on the roof together. "They're getting high," he explained. I imagine he thought the carbon monoxide was intoxicating.

ADDITIONAL SMOKING SOLUTIONS

In addition to ledge removal and making correct screening, there are other strategies that I have referred to but not fully described, which include permanent smoke plates, raising the inner hearth, reducing the size of the whole firebox, and adding chimney height.

PERMANENT SMOKE PLATES

When selecting a smoke plate, it must be decided if it will be temporary or permanent. I consider the economical 4" spring-loaded plate described in Chapter I temporary. A permanent smoke plate would typically be made by a welding shop to exactly your specifications and mounted in place with masonry anchors. (Make sure to first perform the aluminum foil test more than once to determine the right size.) As you can see from the drawing below, I favor flexible tabs spot-welded on the back in order to unobtrusively anchor the plate to the brick. But pieces of 2" x 2" angle iron welded on the back at each end are also an option. Holes are drilled in the angle iron where it can be anchored to the shoulder brick of the sidewall. The plate is typically made of 1/8" boilerplate steel. See Figure 38.

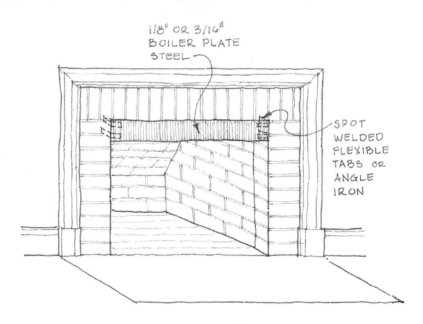

PERMANENT SMOKE PLATE

FIGURE 38

Another style of metal smoke plate, which you may be able to fabricate and install yourself, is mounted *behind* the back of the front brick and mortared in place. This kind of smoke plate is especially appropriate for a deep, *arched* fireplace because most of the smoke is leaking out the top of the arch. Fabrication is easier because tabs or angle iron pieces may not be needed. See Figure 39.

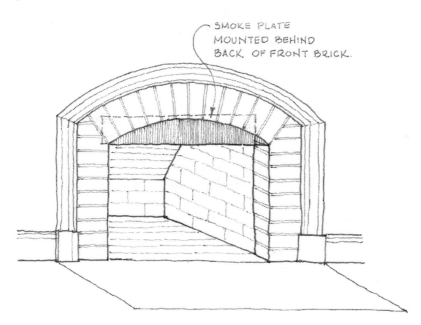

PERMANENT SMOKE PLATE
FOR ARCHED FIREPLACES

FIGURE 39

Notice that the smoke plate in Figure 38 is more or less flush with the front brick while the smoke plate in Figure 39 is installed in a recessed position. I have not noticed any difference in the efficacy of the two locations. For cosmetic reasons, I prefer not to have a smoke plate on the same plane (flush) as the front brick but recessed at least 1" up to 2".

Typically, metal smoke plates are left boiler-plate color, a gray or mottled gray steel, and draw the eye only one time. But they can also be painted a flat black. If you want it painted, I advise you to paint it yourself. A welding shop will always use a *shiny* black no matter what you request. I think shiny black looks tacky.

The advantage of custom-made, permanent smoke plates over factory-made smoke plates is that, in addition to being sized more exactly, they can be installed very *securely*. As you are reaching in to open and close the regular damper, you don't want to be concerned that you may knock the smoke plate loose.

Incidentally, smoke plate *hoods that protrude* beyond the front plane of the fireplace may look authoritative—as if they are actually gathering the smoke—but the hood part is only decorative. It's not actually doing anything. It's the *reduction in the* size of the *front* of the fireplace opening that is corrective.

I need to note here that factory-made smoke plates typically come with a little tube of silicon caulk to help secure the plate in position. In my experience, caulk adds some stability to the installation but not as much as I would like. In any case, I don't like the impression caulk makes. A brick fireplace needs to convey permanence.

RAISING THE INNER HEARTH

Another option for making the fireplace smaller is to raise the inner hearth one or 2 layers of firebrick. You don't even have to mortar the bricks in place although if you plan this as a long-range solution, you would, at a minimum, mortar between the front row bricks with refractory cement. For added stability, refractory might be used on the horizontal surfaces between the old brick and the new. I would not use mortar between the new bricks. But the bricks at the sides will need to be sawed to exact lengths and angles so the whole hearth is really tight. You should use firebrick instead of regular brick because, in addition to holding up to the great heat of the hot coals, they are usually much more uniform. At the end of the job fine sand or firebrick dust (from your sawing) can be swept into the cracks for added stability. See Figure 40.

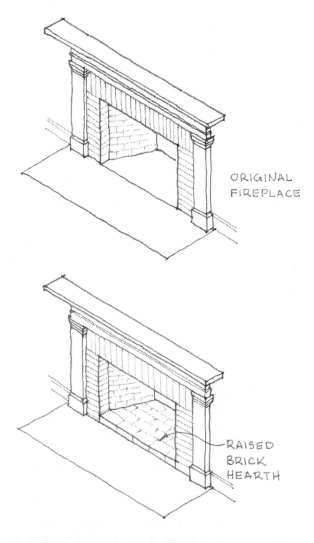

ORIGINAL
FIREPLACE

RAISED
BRICK
HEARTH

RAISING THE
INNER HEARTH

FIGURE 40

Raising the inner hearth is not as effective as a smoke plate because it doesn't also change the *height* of the throat damper in relation to the top of the fireplace opening. This is one of the most common fireplace construction mistakes—not installing the damper at least 6"—preferably 8" to 10"—above the top of the fireplace opening. But raising the inner hearth does achieve the goal of making the whole fireplace *opening* smaller and thereby improving the ratio of fireplace opening to chimney flue.

The main reason I shy away from raising the hearth until I've exhausted all other possibilities is that I don't like the way it looks. Additionally, from a safety standpoint, if the fireplace isn't at least 20 inches deep, there is an increased risk of a burning log rolling out, falling and bouncing onto the flammable floor area beyond the outside hearth. This is one of the reasons for my uneasiness with zero clearance prefab fireplaces, whose inner hearths are always raised six inches.

If you do raise the inner hearth, I strongly recommend you have a good true grate to keep the logs and hot coals trapped inside the firebox.

MAKING THE WHOLE FIREBOX SMALLER

If the ratio is, say, 1 to 20, and glass doors have been ruled out, my first step would probably be to increase the splay. After I'd done that I'd run the aluminum foil test. If I wanted a masonry solution, I'd first install a new lintel. This is most easily done by sawing a piece out of both ends of the right length angle iron— longer than the fireplace is wide. Instead of 3" X 4" angle iron you'd use a smaller size, probably 2" X 2". The ends can then be inserted into a drilled out mortar joint. Brick splits, which are typically half the thickness of regular or firebrick, faced by tile, or stone cut to size fill in the space. I usually parge/stucco the inside surface to give it more strength and stability. See Figure 41.

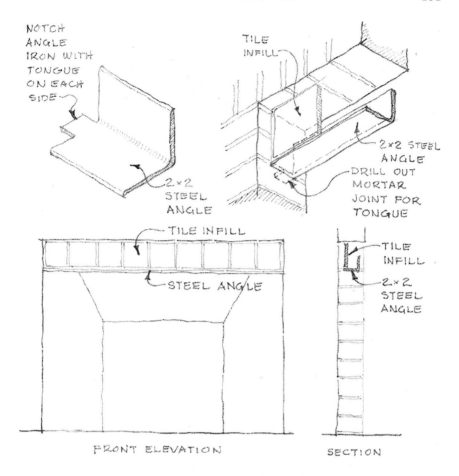

NOTCH ANGLE IRON WITH TONGUE ON EACH SIDE

TILE INFILL

2×2 STEEL ANGLE

2×2 STEEL ANGLE

DRILL OUT MORTAR JOINT FOR TONGUE

TILE INFILL

STEEL ANGLE

TILE INFILL

2×2 STEEL ANGLE

FRONT ELEVATION

SECTION

FIREPLACE TOO TALL THE MASONRY SOLUTION

FIGURE 41

If the firebox needs to be made a great deal smaller, I build what I call a-box-within-a-box—a whole new firebox inside the old one, closing in the sides and the top. In this case, a regular lintel can be used over the top of the fireplace opening because there are new sidewalls to rest it on. See Figure 42.

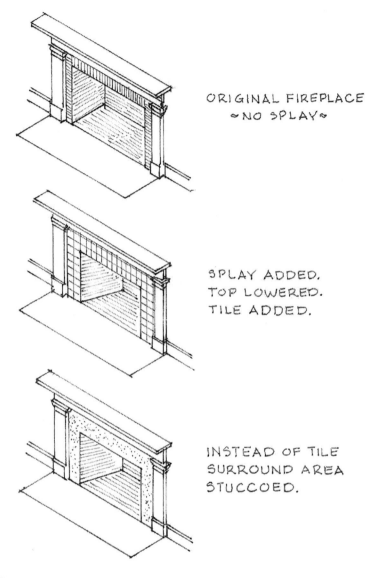

ORIGINAL FIREPLACE
~NO SPLAY~

SPLAY ADDED,
TOP LOWERED.
TILE ADDED.

INSTEAD OF TILE
SURROUND AREA
STUCCOED.

BOX WITHIN A BOX

FIGURE 42

When you build a box within a box, a number of decorative challenges present themselves. Sometimes I have done the simplest thing: parge (i.e., stucco smooth) the new fireplace surround surfaces with mortar or plaster and paint them flat black, in an attempt to make them vanish. Other times, I've added, as I noted above, tile or stone, which can become strong, but natural-looking, visual features. In other words, I feature the correction as if it had been intended solely as a *cosmetic* improvement.

While it may feel unnecessary, it is highly recommended when building (or rebuilding) a fireplace is to test it before adding any kind of finished surround. If it smokes or still smokes, you can make corrections, having run the aluminum foil test to determine what this particular system needs to quit smoking, without having to rip out tile, marble, stucco, etc.

NEW DAMPER CONTROLS OUT OF THIN AIR

A daunting fireplace problem is trying to repair broken damper controls on an existing throat damper, daunting until you grasp the essence of the problem. The key is to understand that a regular damper is a complete machine. There's no point of contact for the controls beyond the damper housing itself. In other words, the bracket that the damper handle intersects with is attached to the damper housing. When the damper controls are broken or hopelessly loose, it's usually the bracket. Reattaching it or replacing it are usually not options because the bolt/nut attaching it to the housing is inaccessibly buried in bricks and mortar behind the front housing. So a new bracket must be fabricated and mounted elsewhere to receive the newly-fashioned damper handle. The simplest strategy is to attach the damper control bracket to the sidewall of the firebox. (The other point of possible attachment is the lintel angle iron.) I have made dozens of these new systems, most of them attached to the sidewall. Usually they end up more user-friendly than the original controls, mainly because you can easily see and reach the handle sliding up and down in the bracket on the side wall. See Figure 43.

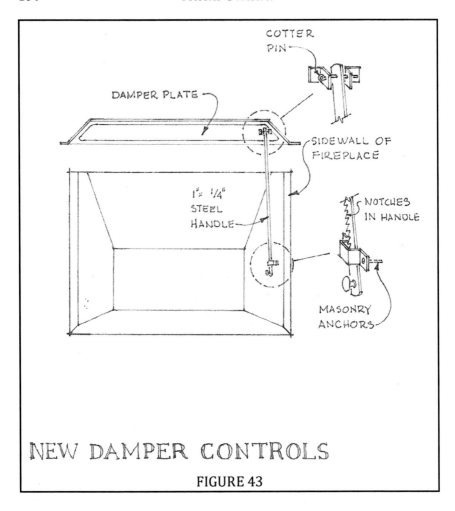

NEW DAMPER CONTROLS

FIGURE 43

ADDING TO CHIMNEY HEIGHT

Another way to make a fireplace stronger is by increasing the height of its chimney. But it does not affect the draw in direct proportion. If you add 10% to the *total* height, you only increase the draw by 5%. Thus, with a very short chimney, adding four or five feet can make a real difference, but if the chimney is already fairly tall, four or five feet won't help much. See Figure 44.

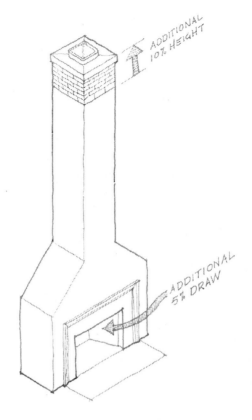

ADDING HEIGHT TO
A SHORT CHIMNEY

FIGURE 44

The problem with adding lots of height to a chimney is that it becomes unstable, especially in high winds, as I explained in Chapter III. Building codes, for good reason, do not permit chimneys to extend more than 10 feet above the roof they start from. Adding height to a chimney is also one of the most expensive smoking fixes.

There may be a different kind of reason, however, to add a little height. I once consulted on a smoking problem at a hotel. They had wood-burning fireplaces on the first floor of their 10-story building. On the roof they also had air intakes for the dining room and the kitchen. What was happening was some of the wood smoke was being pulled down the air intakes. I advised them to add 4' of height to the chimneys. It worked.

WHY FIREPLACES NEED STABILITY

One of my rules for fireplaces (and chimneys) is that nothing should be loose or unstable and capable of falling down or collapsing, especially during a fire. In the extreme case, loose bricks inside a fireplace can fall down and conceivably knock burning logs or live sparks beyond the firebox. This is why I rebuild fireboxes or parts of them, if they are unstable. You may imagine that the inside of a fireplace is inherently stable. But that is not true, partly because normal grade mortar is often used in their construction but also because logs are frequently more or less thrown into the firebox during refueling, especially when the fire is really hot. The logs hit or bounce off the walls, loosening all but the best mortar. Over time, this has a cumulative weakening effect. And the firebox, especially the lower back wall, is subject to huge changes in temperature—well over 1500 degrees—every time you have a fire. The invention and use of firebrick starting more than 150 years ago, however, has limited firebox damage from heat. (Firebrick is designed to withstand temperatures of 2000 F and higher, depending on the rating of the brick.) But the mortar must also be up to the task. As I've mentioned before, when I build a fireplace, I use refractory cement, which holds up well at high temperatures and to general abuse, and keeps the firebox stable for many, many years of hard use.

Chimneys also need stability, especially at their tops. One windy, rainy, winter evening a clergyman telephoned me in a fit of great apprehension to report that bricks were being thrown off his chimney top and landing on his garden furniture below. To him, evil forces were definitely on the rampage. When I stopped by the next day and inspected the top, it was clear that a raccoon or perhaps a family of raccoons had just been trying to gain shelter inside his chimney. The screen had been pulled away and many loose bricks had indeed been thrown or pushed off the top. More on raccoons in CHAPTER VIII.

A PROCESS OF ELIMINATION

The way to proceed with an overall diagnosis is by a process of elimination.

Often I will list a fireplace's strengths and weaknesses, sometimes on paper but usually in my head. A certain kind of customer is intrigued to see (and have a record of) the process. Strengths might be—plenty of air, tall chimney, 110 degree splay, OK screen; weaknesses—damper too low and too far back, 1.5" damper housing ledge on back wall, poor ratio of 1 to 16. In a situation like this, I'd probably tackle the ledge first. I'd then run a test with a small fire. If the fireplace still smokes, I'd then run the test with a true grate I always carry around in my van. Just that 4" higher can make a difference. If these steps did not suffice, I'd do the aluminum foil test to learn *how much* the opening needed to be reduced. If the test showed the fireplace very close to not smoking, I might raise the grate with a brick under each leg, one way to test if a raised hearth might be effective. If that succeeded, I'd let the customer choose between smoke plate or raised inner hearth.

Listing a fireplace's strengths and weaknesses is an excellent exercise. If you work in pairs, the process can become even more robust. For training purposes of new sweeps, it's stellar.

The real challenge, of course, is selecting the weakest link, the one that's weakening the fireplace the most and is least expensive to fix.

MORE FIREPLACE MYTHS DISPELLED

One of the goals of this book is to dispel various fireplace myths, of which there are many. Believing these myths tends to distract from any attempt to improve fireplaces and their best use. What follows is a review of two of the myths.

One very persistent myth is that a smoking fireplace is signaling that the chimney needs to be cleaned, that there is a build-up of creosote, which is impeding the flow of smoke up the chimney. *This is almost never true.* Repeat: This is almost never true. The only way a fireplace chimney can actually be blocked or severely restricted by creosote is if cords of terrible wood have been burned for years—an unlikely scenario because the fireplace would have smoked so badly—or if an incorrectly installed and operated *airtight stove* had been connected to it. *The usual location where a fireplace chimney can actually be blocked or severely restricted by creosote is at the screen at the top of the chimney,* which I described earlier in this chapter. I've encountered it only a half dozen times.

Another myth is that a smoking fireplace could lead to a chimney fire. (Where there's smoke, there'll soon be fire!) This also is completely false. Smoking fireplaces have causes that are far removed from chimney fires, which are defined as fueled by creosote. In fact, it's extremely unlikely that *a smoking fireplace will ever have even a small chimney fire*, which can only happen if there is a significant accumulation of creosote. Badly smoking fireplaces are rarely used, for obvious reasons. Furthermore, a smoking fireplace won't cause some other kind of fire. In one extraordinary instance, I inspected a smoking fireplace that had been heavily used by a crazy person. One side of the wood mantel was badly charred. But, surprisingly, it hadn't been set on fire.

Yet the chief reason chimney sweeps are contacted by homeowners is that their fireplaces smoke. But they don't always tell you about it, why I'm not sure. Maybe they think the smoking is their fault, which it never is, or, that their fears of their house being set on fire, might possibly be true. Maybe they worry about seeming stupid, which they aren't. It's the fireplace terrain that's murky, confusing and, well, stupid. It is for good reasons that husband and wife rarely agree on the status, care, and operation of their fireplace. In any case, when you first look at a fireplace, your first question to yourself should be, "Does it smoke?" It never hurts to also ask the homeowners. I remember one time I looked at a fireplace with broad, dark smoke stains on the brick and mantel above the fireplace opening and so, almost as a joke, I asked the man of the house in a dead serious tone of voice, if his fireplace smoked. (He had not mentioned this when he had made the appointment.) He became flustered but then blurted, "It smokes in the winter!" That's as far as he would go.

Summary

The best, most versatile test is the aluminum foil test. From information I've described so far, you should be able to build or rebuild the perfect fireplace. When smoking starts is instructive to diagnosing a problem. Incorrectly installed throat dampers almost always contribute to smoke problems. How to make a screen for the top of a chimney. How to make permanent smoke plates. How to make new damper controls. Two more fireplace myths exposed: that a fireplace is smoking because of creosote build-up and needs to be cleaned (NEVER) and that a smoking fireplace could lead to a chimney fire (NEVER).

CHAPTER V

MORE EFFICIENT FIREPLACES

CONTENTS

Biggest flaw: fireplaces are designed to work without smoking right from the start—They almost immediately are drawing too hard, harder than necessary to remove smoke—Top damper can decrease draw of chimney as it heats up—For my test, I installed a temperature probe about 10' above the fireplace to compare chimney temperatures with top damper wide open and with it restricted as much as possible—Hot chimney ratio of fireplace opening area to flue area ended up much, much greater—Results of tests—Also saving energy at end of fire—Best top damper—The 2nd biggest flaw with fireplaces is that none of the heat of the flue gasses is utilized—A Canadian researcher has devised a method for doing this, the one-brick thick chimney breast

It seemed like a normal job. The lady had recently had a baby and planned to stay home during the next year. She wanted to use her fireplace but it had no damper. What was to be done? I recommended a top damper. I actually had the right size in my van. I installed it. As I was leaving I told the woman that she might be able to restrict it when the chimney got hot. I had no idea if she could really do this to any great extent but I showed her how just in case she tried. This was early in my career. I'd just thrown out the idea to make conversation.

Well, fast forward to the next spring. She had called back to have chimney cleaned. She had used it every day during the winter months, she said, burning several cords of wood. As I was setting up my sweeping equipment, I happened to remember that I had told her she might be able to restrict the top damper when the chimney got hot.

"Did you try restricting the top damper?"
"Of course", she replied. "You told me to."

And she then showed me how much she'd been able to restrict it, which turned out to be almost 80%! I was floored. This was far more than I'd imagined possible. It pushed me into a search that two other equally smart customers had actually asked about. Why can't we make a fireplace into a real heater? Intuitively, they figured it must be possible. I hated telling them I didn't know how.

This lady's experience started me on what became a 10-year project to replicate her results and hopefully improve on them. My first step was to devise a protocol. By installing a heat probe inside the flue some 10' above the fireplace I realized I could determine that top damper restriction was actually *reducing* the amount of house air also being drawn up the chimney. *If the probe's thermometer registered a higher temperature when I restricted the top damper, I reasoned that I was restricting house air, not the much hotter combustion gasses.* House air is always hundreds of degrees cooler. At the same time, of course, I was also monitoring any smoking. I didn't want to restrict the damper so much that I caused smoke to leak out of the fireplace opening. I simply wanted to *reduce* the amount of house air also being drawn up the chimney.

The theoretical basis for this protocol was a graph I had commissioned which plotted smoke/gas velocity against temperature.

A chimney that starts out cold, according to the graph, typically drawing at about .8'/second, may end up, when well heated, drawing as much as 32'/second, a 40-fold increase. But it's not only increasing the velocity of the smoke going up the chimney. The increased velocity translates into *increased volume*. As the volume of smoke or hot gasses is more or less constant, large quantities of *house air* end up being also drawn into the fireplace, needlessly it became clear, out of the house, up the chimney, and thrown away to the great outdoors. See Figure 4 again, which I showed you in Chapter I.

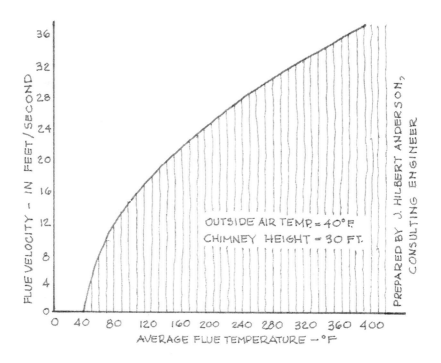

RELATIONSHIP BETWEEN
CHIMNEY TEMPERATURE AND
SMOKE / GAS VELOCITY

FIGURE 4

As if this were not bad enough—this loss of heated house air—it also results in a reduction of air pressure in the house and outside air begins to seep in at every crack it can find to *displace* the lost house air, in effect cooling the whole house. In fact, the only part of the house, which typically ends up being warmed, is the room with the fireplace. (You may have noticed this phenomenon when you had a long fire.) With extremely strong chimneys or on very cold days, even the room with the fireplace is cooled. In the worst cases, as I have mentioned with a very tight house, house air becomes so depleted that outside cold air *begins coming down* the hot chimney, momentarily causing the fireplace to smoke. This reversal stops as soon as air pressure inside the house is sufficiently restored.

Another way of describing the cooling effect is that fireplace use can significantly increase the rate of outside air infiltration, i.e., the number of air changes per hour, at least doubling it and sometimes more than quadrupling it. (The usual rate of air changes is 1 to 3 times/hour.) While this may not be very important in relatively mild Washington, DC, it's extremely important a couple of hundred miles to the north and, increasingly so, in really cold regions or on very cold days.

It's hard to grasp the full picture from a heating perspective but I believe between $1/3^{rd}$ and $2/3^{rd}$'s of what's typically being pulled up a hot chimney and thrown away is house air. (The good thing is that the air inside the house becomes very fresh and very salubrious...!)

For the record, I noticed that restricting the top damper even beyond the point where the fireplace begins to smoke a little increased chimney flue temperatures very significantly. I wish I could figure out a way to take advantage of this.

It turned out that quite precise adjustments were needed when the top damper was restricted. I describe the controls of various top dampers in a moment and the one that I selected. But this was quite an involved process because, initially, I was forced to fashion my own controls in order to reach the precision needed.

Below is a summary of results from hundreds of tests. The consistency of the results was compelling: flue restriction with top dampers clearly works.

With the top damper wide open, the heat probe registered almost 450 degrees F. With it restricted as much as possible, the flue temperature rose to 630 degrees. This test was conducted at my house in Washington, DC. When I'd climb onto the roof and measure how open the damper plate when restricted was, it was less than ¾"! According to my calculations, which include allowing for the resistance created by the right angle turn at the damper plate, this translates into a fireplace/flue ratio of more than 1 to 40, or more than triple 1 to 12. I can see that there are many other ways these calculations could be made, which would probably lead to somewhat different numbers. But the benefit of significant damper restriction is clear, which could lead to much less wasteful fireplace operation.

To get the best results, i.e., when the greatest restriction is possible, you need a big fire that fills the firebox. To get the fire hot as quickly as possible, I had split the firewood into sticklike pieces between ½" and 1" thick. When these were burning well, I began adding larger pieces up to 2". When the flue temperatures began to exceed 300 F, I started restricting the top damper. During the final stages I would begin adding 3" logs and, when those were burning well, start restricting the top damper more. Even a little top damper restriction beyond half-closed seemed to modestly accelerate the heating of the chimney.

Needless to say, it is absolutely necessary to be burning seasoned wood, which ignites immediately. To insure quick heat and nearly complete combustion as soon as possible, it's not a bad idea, at the beginning of the fire, to use one or more of those quick start wafers. See Chapter XI.

The other testing device I had were regular house thermometers, which I'd placed in the rooms upstairs, which were relatively airtight. With the top damper wide-open, temperatures upstairs kept falling, about one degree an hour, down to ambient outdoor temperatures. *With the top damper restricted, they didn't budge during a 3-hour fire.*

The most noticeable change with the top damper restricted is that the flames stayed in the firebox longer, actually slowing down their rush up the chimney. Although the room got fairly toasty when I was not using the top damper, it got noticeably more toasty when I was using it. There were probably two causes for this. The first was that the fireplace was actually pumping out more heat. The room was actually a lot hotter. The other was that the fireplace was drawing much less air, which of course normally ends up cooling both the firebox itself, the fireplace room, as well as the whole house. My fuel lasted longer.

I couldn't figure out how to accurately measure the amount of heat being radiated by the fireplace in the two different modes of operation. I consider this a serious flaw. But the comparative flue temperatures are compelling: *a hot fireplace chimney can be significantly restricted without creating a smoking problem.*

I had not installed any outside air intakes, no Condars, no basement outside air intake, mainly because the house was only airtight upstairs, while on the 1st floor—where the fireplace was—there were 3 somewhat leaky doors to the outside.

I have run this same test in a house in Jacksonville, FL. The results were similar. With the top damper open, I could usually reach 480 degrees F; with it restricted I was at more than 680.

The two fireplaces had differences. The Washington fireplace only had splay of 110 degrees. The Jacksonville fireplace had 120, which may explain the higher temperatures. The Washington chimney was 22 feet high, the Jacksonville chimney 33 feet. Ambient temperature in Washington was 50 degrees. In Jacksonville, it was 75, another possible contributor to the higher flue temperatures. I did not bother putting thermometers all over the house in Jacksonville because it was leaky on all 3 floors. Both chimneys were interior.

Because I didn't have access to the top of the Jacksonville chimney, I'd installed a Drop-In RMR damper where the chimney went through the attic. So I have no comparable measurement to the ¾" opening I was able to achieve at the top of the Washington chimney.

When I checked my test chimney in Washington for creosote after burning about 2 cords of wood, it was absolutely spotless. There were no deposits at all. Same with the chimney in Jacksonville. I attribute this to nearly total combustion of the smoke. Additionally, higher flue temperatures prevent creosote deposition. Interior chimneys, which are naturally warmer for being inside the house, tend to have much less creosote if any.

I tried for years in Washington to achieve similar results with a *regular throat damper using rotary controls*, which would have even more precise adjustments than the best top dampers. See Figure 45.

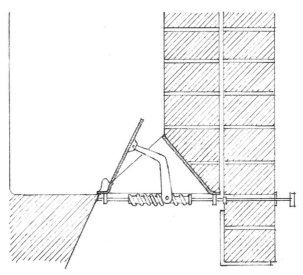

ROTARY CONTROL
THROAT DAMPER

FIGURE 45

I was unsuccessful. I could restrict the lower damper half-way—down to a 2" opening from a 4" opening—but the heat probe registered *no temperature increase at all in the chimney* and the house thermometer readings upstairs kept dropping. If I restricted it more than half, I began to get results but then the fireplace started smoking, if only minimally. This is the big flaw with a fireplace that has no top damper.

My theory for why a restricted top damper is so effective is that the hottest gas molecules must rise faster in their trip up the chimney flue than the house air molecules. I wish I knew exactly what's happening inside those flues.

VARIABLES AFFECTING CHIMNEY OPERATION
Chimney temperature is the largest variable determining chimney draw.

Outside ambient temperature, i.e., temperature of outside air at the top of the chimney, shown on the graph as 76 degrees, also plays a part. The graph only shows chimney temperature increase affecting velocity. But if it's very cold outside, your chimney will draw much harder because there's an even greater temperature difference between the gasses in the fireplace and the outside air at the top of the chimney. For example, when outside temperatures fall from 50 degrees to zero, the draw of a chimney doubles! This is a reason not to use your fireplace on a very cold day because the chimney will draw even harder and will end up cooling the rest of your house even more than usual.

A different kind of variable for fireplace systems is the degree of splay of the sidewalls, which determines the air pressure difference. As I've said, a one-degree increase in the angle of each sidewall (starting at 100 degrees) will translate into at least a 1% increase in chimney draw/draft.

A third variable is the ratio of flue size to fireplace opening. A fireplace system with a ratio of 1 to 8 is going to draw a greater percentage of house air than one with a ratio of 1 to 18. (Assuming both are non-smoking fireplaces, the fireplace with the 1 to 8 ratio will draw far more house air.)

Yet another variable is the height of the chimney. Doubling total chimney height increases chimney draw by about 50%. A 50' tall chimney, for example, is going to draw 50% harder than a 25' chimney.

The larger point I'm making is that the official ratios between fireplace opening and flue size are not at all precise and can vary tremendously even within a particular fireplace system. And these variations can be very costly in terms of energy efficiency.

For example, let's examine a particularly exaggerated hypothetical case. We have a 50-foot tall chimney. It's interior and therefore always warm. It's a cold day, around 20 degrees F. The splay of the sidewalls is 120 degrees. The ratio for this hypothetical fireplace/ chimney system will theoretically be more than one to 40, a far cry from one to 12, the officially recommended ratio. Using such a fireplace will really, really cool the house. Even using it on a 50-degree F. day will seriously cool the house.

My point is that fireplaces without top dampers and good controls are far less efficient than they could be.

An even greater splay of the sidewalls, say 135 degrees, could increase heat output further because the top damper could be restricted more and the 135 degree splays would radiate more heat. Even increasing the splay to 125 or 130 degrees should increase heat output.

Others should perform their own tests to verify my results or at least their general direction. I wouldn't be surprised if my basic test methodology—the heat probe measuring the flue temperature—can be improved upon.

To remind you, I found that when using restricted top dampers on fireplaces I had built, the *fireplace/flue ratio* increased from 12 to 1 to between 30 to 1 and 40 to 1, that is, between 2.5 and almost 3.5 times

These tests (and others) should be run, the results put side by side, and then the capital and labor costs of constructing the various designs and efficiencies compared.

TESTING FOR CORRECT RESTRICTION

The way to determine proper top damper closure during a fire is to *sniff* or otherwise monitor along the top of the fireplace opening, the place where smoking is going to occur, just as we did in the aluminum foil smoke test. You begin to close the damper an inch at a time at first and then, after 3 inches, in as small increments as the damper controls permit. As in the smoke test, if you smell *anything*, even heat, the fireplace is smoking. Immediately retreat until you smell nothing. If you don't like using your nose, as I've mentioned earlier, the gas grill igniter works great in this application because it's so easily lit and can be made to stay lit. I hold its flame against the bottom of the steel lintel. As long as the flame is drawn *into* the firebox, the fireplace is not smoking.

You should not attempt restriction until the fire is burning brightly and very little smoke *as smoke* is visible. I aim for about 8 minutes into an average fire, if you're burning seasoned, split sticklike fuel to start with. At least 85% of what is leaving the firebox should be hot clear gases, very little smoke. (For a solid fuel to burn, 2 steps must take place: the fuel must be heated enough to become gaseous, i.e., smoke. The next step is that this gas, or smoke, burns. The latter step is what gives off heat. The first step, vaporization, requires heat input.)

If you're having smoky smoldering fires and are never able to consume most of the smoke, your wood is either green or rotten, i.e., filled with sap or rainwater. Or your logs are too big and should be split into three-inch diameter pieces or even smaller. Later in the fire, when you have a big bed of hot coals, somewhat larger logs, if well seasoned, can be used.

A smoky fire does no heating and will even more seriously cool the house, not even heating the room with the fireplace. It also pollutes the atmosphere.

Once the top damper has been set in its most restricted mode for a fire, it probably won't need resetting for that particular fire unless you're having a really long fire—more than four hours.

And every time you have a fire, I have found that the final setting ends up the same. In other words, you shouldn't, once you have the routine down, have to repeat the sniff or gas igniter test every time. Use a magic marker on the sidewall right below the bottom of the (ball) chain damper controls to designate when the opening is correct.

AT THE END OF THE FIRE

There is another important moment to change the setting of the top damper—as the fire is dying down and there are no flames or only very low flames and mostly a bed of hot coals. Again, you might use your nose or the gas grill igniter as the testing device: close the top damper all the way—it should make a thunking or shutter sound—and then open it as little as possible. Sniff as you did before at the top of the fireplace opening. If you smell *anything*, even just that hot smell, back off another notch. You should only need a slit between ¼" and 3/8" opening at the top of the chimney.

If restricting the damper *during a fire* is too scary, start off with restricting it only at the end of a fire. (You may need a thermally insulated glove to safely manipulate the controls at the end of a long hot fire.) If you use your fireplace a lot, this practice—end-of-fire restriction—can pay for the top damper in a year.

The reason you want a little chimney draw all night is because the hot coals are giving off some carbon monoxide. Also, if you close the damper all the way while you still have hot coals, the house will smell the next day.

Remember to close both dampers completely when you get up in the morning.

Notice that the use of a top damper mainly helps homeowners lose less house air. A secondary, slightly less dramatic effect, is that the fireplace is actually radiating more heat. But combining the two effects can make an important difference to fireplace efficiency, probably doubling it.

CHOOSING THE BEST TOP DAMPER

I favor the RMR ball chain controls because the balls are only ¼" apart, which allow for quite precise adjustments. The user-friendly (but obtrusive) tripod, lever control mechanism of the Chimalator top damper, on the other hand, has adjustments only every ¾" inch. The regular chain controls on other top dampers, fall in between, about ½". While RMR has several top damper designs, most of them a plate that goes up and down, it also has a butterfly design and a weighted swivel design, the Drop-In top damper. I have not yet run the tests comparing the efficacy of the different damper designs. Unlike the damper controls, I suspect the RMR dampers themselves are roughly comparable to other dampers. Speaking of top damper controls, I've always wondered if generic, user-friendly, efficient controls could be invented. The challenge will be to accommodate the different spring strengths that keep these dampers open. For instance, the Chimalator springs are very strong, a good thing because any top damper plate can get stuck shut over the summer months or if bad wood has been used. Chimalator's lever controls always work fine even under extreme conditions. Other top dampers have much less powerful springs and are less dependable. I once tried RMR controls on a Chimalator top damper. They proved almost impossible to manipulate with one hand.

SAFETY CONCERNS WITH TOP DAMPER USE

A possible safety problem is that restricting the top damper could increase chimney temperature, not only on the inside of the chimney but on the outside of the chimney as well. If your chimney is not lined, however, with terra cotta or perhaps with stainless steel—90% of fireplace chimneys in the USA are lined—it is very likely that using a top damper during a fire will overheat the chimney and set nearby wood on fire. But, assuming you have a lined chimney, I consider this scenario unlikely. My Washington test chimney was lined with terra cotta inside 4"(actually 3.5") cement block and got slightly warm for a few inches right below the top damper. (The roof was 4 feet below.) But because masonry chimneys are all built differently, I would advise, to confirm chimney safety, checking the temperature of the outside of the chimney inside the house when you have a regular fire and then when using the top damper for several hours in the most restricted mode. Where the chimney goes through the attic is an ideal location for monitoring temperature because it's often exposed. Interior chimneys, for obvious reasons, are more likely to have wood nearby and need closer monitoring than exterior chimneys.

(For the record, the Jacksonville chimney got relatively hot, about 150 degrees, right below the Drop-In Damper. Two feet below that, at attic floor level, the chimney never heated up.)

Experience may show us that chimney flues need to be insulated for reasons of safety if you are having long fires with a top damper maximally restricted. One ideal situation, however, would be for interior chimneys especially to become heat repositories— thermal mass batteries, as it were. They would be insulated wherever there were combustibles near by but otherwise free to radiate stored heat.

If there is a hazard with being able to really use your fireplace as a heater, it's probably more likely to be caused by the ever-growing bed of hot coals on the inner hearth, as I describe in the next chapter, RISK FACTORS, and the likely longer duration of fires. If you've never had big, long fires in your old fireplace, get your chimney sweep to determine that there is no combustible material anywhere near the hearth or back wall. Most of these defective installations should be immediately noticeable to a professional. I have more information on fireplace safety inspections in the next chapter.

For very long fires, where there is a deep build-up of hot coals, *log rests* without andirons may be the best strategy. These are made of the high-grade cast iron and will not melt at even the highest temperatures. See Figure 46.

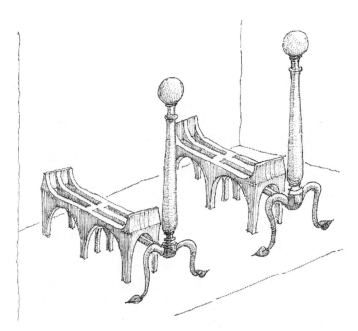

THE DONLEY LOG REST

FIGURE 46

Remember, in the first chapter, my story of the man who set his house on fire? Although there were other elements involved, *long duration of the fire* was a critical risk factor. A *brief* fire in "my cowboy's" fireplace with the glass doors closed would, as I pointed out, not have caused any problem.

The other thing that can go wrong is that restricting the top damper increases *the pressure* inside the chimney and may force smoke/gases to leak through a wall or into an abutting flue. I've only had this happen on two separate jobs. As a general rule, the pressure inside an operating chimney flue is lower than inside the house and will therefore be *pulling air into it* rather than leaking smoke out. This seems to be true even when the top damper is maximally restricted.

In new construction, the possibility of crossover is another reason to completely isolate the flues from each other with an airtight wythe between the flues.

TAPPING THE HEAT OF THE FLUE GASSES

None of my proposals have made use of the flue gas heat except in the most general way—treating the chimney as a heat storage battery. But there is a more direct way for this that was developed and tested by David J.N. Warren, a former associate for the Centre for Research and Development in Masonry, Calgary, Alberta, Canada, in the late 1970's and early 1980's. Warren's main finding was that fireplaces *with a single brick depth above the fireplace opening*—i.e., the smoke chamber—were twice as efficient as fireplaces with thicker chimney breast walls, double or triple brick thickness, the usual construction pattern. I'd also noticed increased heat with this design on several occasions but didn't grasp its potential significance. (The other changes Warren made were to increase the firebox sidewall splay from 105 to more than 125 degrees; to decrease fireplace depth from 20.5" to 17"; to increase the height of the opening, i.e., to make the fireplace larger and square, as Rumford had proposed; and lastly to install a top damper to be closed when the fireplace was not in use.)

Part of the cause of this extra thickness of the chimneybreast is the design of many dampers now in use, which, to create a throat, includes an angled, hooded portion at the front of the housing to the tune of some 4". See side view of the damper housing, Figure 47.

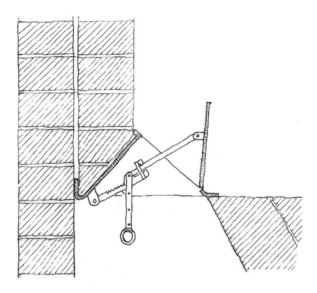

TYPICAL THROAT DAMPER DESIGN

FIGURE 47

Fireplaces without a *thick* chimneybreast can, however, create a problem for pictures, especially paintings, hung on that wall over the fireplace. They end up fried. I consider the thick chimneybreast one of those instances where convenience—making the space above the fireplace completely safe for wall decoration like paintings—won out over heat output, efficiency.

See profiles of conventional fireplaces and energy efficient (modified) fireplaces, Figure 48. I would start the flue liners higher than is shown in the drawings and I would include a smoke chamber in the energy efficient fireplace.

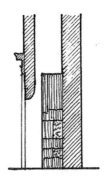

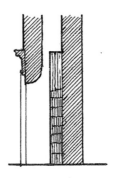

SKINNY AND FAT
CHIMNEY BREASTS

FIGURE 48

Now see the temperature readings on the chimneybreasts of a conventional fireplace and of a modified fireplace during a fire, Figure 49.

Fig. 2.11 Modified Fireplace Surface Temperatures

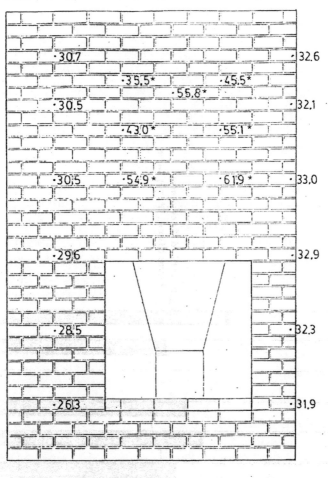

Ambient Air Temperature = 33.8°C

SURFACE TEMPERATURES 2 HOURS AND
10 MINUTES AFTER FIRE WAS LIT

FIGURE 49

Immediately above the fireplace, temperatures are double.

The use of a top damper during fires, as I've described, could further increase the temperatures shown in Warren's modified fireplace, possibly very significantly, depending on a number of factors, especially how much of the smoke chamber can be utilized to collect and radiate heat into the house.

Difficulties in Utilization of Top Dampers
Warren's failure to understand that top dampers can be restricted during a fire and prevent some loss of house air, while regrettable, is understandable. One of the issues he may not have grasped is obvious in the graph I've shown plotting flue temperature and gas velocity inside a chimney. The initial variations in velocity are huge, much larger than anyone would expect. The other illusive issue is how extremely small changes in top damper settings affect the overall dynamic. I remember running an early test using a Chimalator top damper with its degrees of closure every ¾". I got no results at all. Then I fashioned new controls so I could fine-tune damper closure and I began to get results: much higher flue temperatures without smoking. But this equipment and these experiments took me years. I had many false starts. Close familiarity with most of the available equipment was a big help. Another advantage I had was that there were far more top damper designs—and more control possibilities—than when Warren was doing his experiments. I have recently tried to track him down with no success.

Looking back in history, trapping heat from flue gasses was done with the Roman Hypocaust, the Korean Ondol, the Afghan Tawakhaneh, the Chinese K'ang and probably many others now lost to the mists of time. In each case flue heat was circulated under the floor. Later solutions to trapping flue gas heat can be seen with the 90% efficient European masonry stove. For those interested in finding out about these remarkable stoves, go to www.mha-net.org.

What the top damper makes possible is for an open fireplace to trap more of the flue gas heat because there is less cooling of the flue gasses by house air.

In building such a fireplace, it's important to expand the smoke chamber as much as possible, making it wider and taller than normal. The goal is to increase the amount of surface area capable of absorbing flue gas heat, which in turn will radiate through the one layer of brick into the house.

In addition to extracting heat from the flue gasses during a fire, the chimneybreast will continue to radiate heat long after the fire has died down.

Insulating the three other sides of the smoke chamber is necessary if the chimney is exterior to the house. According to the tests I've done, temperatures inside the smoke chamber eventually top out around 500 degrees F. Most of the heat radiating into the room will range from 200 to 300 degrees from a 3-hour fire. Longer fires may initially increase these temperatures.

If cracking at the mortar joints proves to be a problem, it can probably be prevented by using especially good fireclay mortar. And if that still doesn't do the job, the operative parts of the smoke chamber will have to be made with firebrick, which adds some expense. I would be inclined to lay the firebrick on edge, which decreases the thickness of the wall from 4.5" to 2.25".

Harnessing the smoke chamber to increase fireplace output is new, unexplored territory but is probably the best way to have both *an open fire* and a much more efficient fireplace. I wish I were a younger man and could see this through.

These fireplaces are going to look more modern than most traditional fireplaces, which usually sport wood mantels, i.e., flammable mantels. Perhaps the parts of the smoke chamber facing the room and radiating heat would be tiled.

IMPORTANCE OF INSULATING THE FIREBOX

To insure that as much of the fireplace heat as possible is radiated into the room, either from the fireplace itself or with the single brick smoke chamber if that is part of your system, it's vital that the firebox be carefully insulated. I often use a high temperature insulating board or split insulating bricks for behind the lower back wall bricks, the hottest part of the firebox, and, then, higher up and behind the splayed side walls, where I have more room, a coarse vermiculite/Portland mix, moistened but still pourable. (While not as effective as insulating board or insulating bricks, it's far cheaper.) (Perlite or Permalite can also be used if vermiculite is not available. Rock wool insulation, a rather expensive alternative for this job, will also work.) See Figure 50.

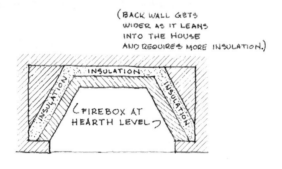

INSULATING THE FIREBOX

FIGURE 50

A typical firebox is not intentionally insulated at all. Masonry trash is simply thrown in behind the firebrick. This obviously conducts heat fairly well to the surrounding masonry, exactly what we don't want.

If we are also tapping flue gas heat via the smoke chamber, we must insulate the parts of the smoke chamber that are not inside the house. We must also determine that there are no nearby combustibles.

THE FUNCTION OF SPLAY

Not only does good splay—above 110 degrees—make fireplaces draw harder, good splay also radiates more heat into the room, Rumford's chief motive for greater splay. See Figure 51.

FIREPLACE WITH
GOOD SPLAY

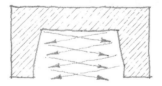

TYPICAL FIREPLACE

GOOD SPLAY
RADIATES MORE HEAT
FIGURE 51

(Without the use of a top damper, increased splay may be self-defeating: although the splay will radiate more heat into the house, it may also make the chimney hotter and increase its draw, pulling even more air out of the house along with the smoke and gasses. Outside air intakes, especially the Condar, will blunt the impact of increased splay but won't be nearly as effective as a restricted top damper. Experience may show us that we want both.)

To increase the amount and temperature of radiant heat, it is also imperative that the brick surfaces inside the fireplace and at the chimneybreast be *as hot as possible*. For example, if surfaces are 100 degrees F, the total heat transfer—heat radiated—is 47 BTU's/hour/square foot. If surfaces are 600 degrees, the transfer is 2,620 BTU's/hour, an exponential increase.

The problem with a fireplace at higher temperatures is that the firebrick *absorb* heat as well as radiating it. This is the reason that I favor building fireboxes with the bricks laid on the narrow side, giving us a brick thickness of 2.25" rather than one 4.5", which is their thickness on the flat. The high temperatures I achieve in my fireplaces require that I construct the firebox using *refractory* cement not regular or even Portland cement and fireclay. See Figure 52.

The other modification of the firebox is to *step* the back wall. See two possible ways I have done that. Stepping the bricks, usually with a lip of ¾" to 1" always increases the height of the *burned-clean-crescent* on the back wall. It also increases *turbulence* on the back wall, which insures a more complete burn, i.e., more of the smoke is actually consumed before it is pulled out of the burn zone—up the chimney. See Figure 53.

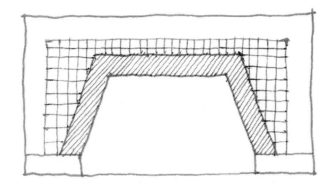

FIREBRICKS ON FLAT

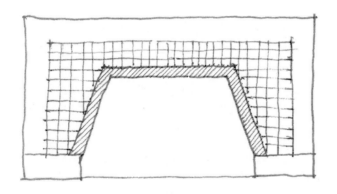

FIREBRICKS ON SIDES

THICKNESS OF FIREBRICKS

FIGURE 52

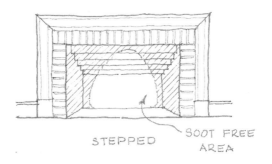

STEPPED   SOOT FREE AREA

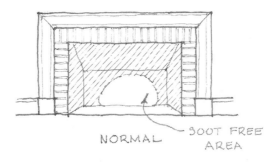

NORMAL   SOOT FREE AREA

STEPPED FIREPLACE BURNS HOTTER
FIGURE 53

There are a number of ways to step the back wall. The main goal is to add *modest impediments* to the flow of gasses being drawn up the chimney and leave more heat behind in the firebox, which will be radiated into the room. Sometimes I've used firebrick splits (1.25" thick) to create more steps. Whatever you do to get steps, there's inevitably lots of sawing.

Stepping the back wall also enables the fireplace builder to lace or overlap brick at the two back corners of the firebox, which is virtually impossible to do in a consistent way with a *sloping or pitched* back wall. Lacing or overlapping at the corners makes the whole firebox much, much more stable.

An additional plus with stepping the fireplace is that the stepped bricks absorb more heat, get hotter and then emit more radiant heat *horizontally* rather than downwards. See Figure 54.

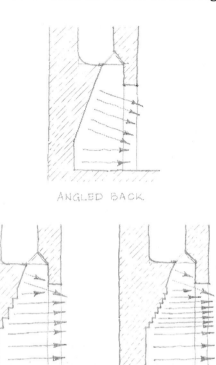

ANGLED BACK.

FULL STEPS   SPLIT STEPS

RADIATION PATTERNS

FIGURE 54

The greater the pitch of the back wall, the more heat is trapped and radiated into the room. *Remember that no amount of back wall pitch (or steps) ever caused a fireplace to smoke.* The only time my steps created a problem was near the back of the throat damper housing. I now quit my steps 8" below the damper.

THE TOP DAMPER COULD HELP IN AN EMERGENCY
In the event of a blackout, when central heaters can't operate, fireplaces outfitted with top dampers could be used to heat one or two rooms. Even in very cold weather, I think indoor temperatures of 60 to 70 degrees are probably achievable. But, for best results, these rooms must be designed so they can be sealed off from the rest of the house. In new construction it may be wise to insulate their interior walls, ceilings, and floors. So instead of being concerned with comfort when there's no central heating, we can save our concern for when the temperatures approach freezing. It would be more like the old days where most of our houses were more or less unheated.

It may be necessary to install some kind of outside air intake to this closed space to keep the fire going because it will be a closed space within a closed space.

My other idea is that using a good top damper could delay how soon we feel we must turn on our central heating at the beginning of the heating season and how soon we can turn it off as spring approaches. An efficient fireplace, plus a warm sweater, should shorten the heating season. I think households could make a game of this—reducing your carbon footprint with your fireplace.

STEPS TO INCREASE EFFICIENCY

- Install top damper, preferably with the ball chain controls. Route the cable through the lower damper housing. Close both dampers when fireplace is not in use.
- Restrict top damper during fires and at the end of fires.
- Get the fire up and running hard as fast as you can.
- Have big, long fires to make the firebox as hot as possible. A big fire is significantly more efficient than a small or medium-sized fire. Don't skimp on adding fuel frequently. (And don't be cavalier about staying in full attendance!)

If firebox reconstruction is an option or if it's new construction, there are additional possible modifications:

- Increase splay of sidewalls to between 120 and 130 degrees, if the fireplace is wide enough to accommodate the increase. Unless you have a special source of wood, or cut it yourself, the back wall should never be less than 18" wide and preferably 20"-24".
- Insulate the firebox as described above.
- Make the chimneybreast/smoke chamber above the fireplace opening into a radiator by constructing it only one brick thick. Between this and top damper restriction, total heat output can be greatly increased.

SUMMARY

Depending on where we're starting, most fireplaces could increase their heat output and efficiency several times over. Because of higher fireplace and chimney temperatures, there will be little or no creosote deposition in the flues, lessening the possibility of chimney fires and decreasing and probably eliminating the need for chimney sweeping. Reduced air pollution because of almost zero particulates (i.e., smoke) escaping from the firebox is definitely possible. Peace of mind, well, relative peace of mind, is also attainable knowing you have an alternative source of heat. If your electricity goes out, as I've mentioned, so does your furnace or boiler. With the one-brick chimneybreast and a good top damper, you're entering, although modestly, into the realm of an open fire heating machine, a poor man's masonry stove

CHAPTER VI

RISK FACTORS

CONTENTS

Fireplaces much less risky than public believes—The risks of cooking and candles are much greater—Virtually no risk of death from failing to sweep fireplace chimneys—Dangers of carbon monoxide—Dangers of hearth fires caused by regular fires of long duration—How to do a fireplace safety inspection

The first point to make about *masonry* fireplaces is that, if built to code and operated with forethought, attentiveness, and good wood, the risks are almost non-existent.

It's probably safer, as I've said, to crank up your fireplace with a big fire than to drive a couple miles to the supermarket. There are fewer variables. There are fewer factors not completely under your control.

I don't want to give home cooking—one of man's most noble activities and my favorite—a bad name but lots of deaths and serious fires take place in the kitchen! Candles (!) kill hundreds of people in the United States every year. Smoking cigarettes in bed is a very bad idea for more than one reason... Compare the risks of these activities against those of fireplaces and fireplaces always win hands down.

From 2004 to 2011 there were no deaths for failing to clean a fireplace chimney, according to a surprising statement in the 2012 report by the National Fire Protection Association (NFPA). So chimney sweeping usually does not prevent loss of life. (I consider sweeping useful, as I've said earlier, because big chimney fires potentially shorten the lives of terra cotta flue liners and stainless steel liners.)

Wood stoves and their connectors are far more dangerous than fireplace chimneys, even dirty ones. Six of the reported deaths were caused by an issue I am discussing later in this chapter. Space heaters were a problem. "In the 2006-2010 period, portable or fixed space heaters, including wood stoves were involved in one-third (32%) of home heating fires and four out of five (80%) home heating deaths," according to NFPA's estimates of "Home Heating Fires-2011." Note that fireplaces were not even mentioned.

There were no injuries from fireplaces in 2002 and 30 injuries in 2003, the latter anomalous, way too high. From 2004 to 2011, no injuries at all from fireplaces were reported. Only 4 percent of home heating property damage came from fireplaces. The way I read these statistics is that homeowners are usually present during fireplace use. Quick action was taken when things went awry.

To put this in perspective, there are an average of 500 deaths per year in the home from carbon monoxide poisoning, most of them from home heating equipment.

CARBON MONOXIDE POISONINGS
When I first started my chimney business in Washington, DC in the late 1970's, there was a tragic front page news story about a carbon monoxide poisoning. After the gas company had turned off

the gas-fired boiler in a rental property on Capitol Hill in January, the man of the house, a construction worker, had turned it on again. A little knowledge is... To reduce their gas bill, his wife and he had put clear plastic over all the windows inside. Within three weeks after turning the boiler back on, she and their three small children were dead. They stayed inside—indoors—almost all the time. The construction worker found them when he came home from work. He was reported as saying it must have been an "act of God," which it clearly was not.

Knowing what I know about Washington slumlords, who always delay fixing anything and usually evict any tenant who reports any kind of problem, there was more than enough blame to go around. Our local gas company should have also been held responsible. I bet you I could have made that boiler chimney function safely in less than 4 minutes.

The problem is as follows. A typical installation has the pipe from the boiler or furnace going into the chimney as shown below. Where the chimney can get blocked is at the elbow at the base of the chimney. Chimney sweeps know to check this elbow and clean out any debris that has accumulated. New codes in many jurisdictions call for an open space or pit directly below the elbow. An ideal installation, in my view, would have a cast iron cleanout door right below the elbow, giving easy access to the pit. What I have found at the elbow are mainly leaves and bits and pieces of decaying chimney. Over many years of neglect these can accumulate enough to block the elbow. See Figure 55

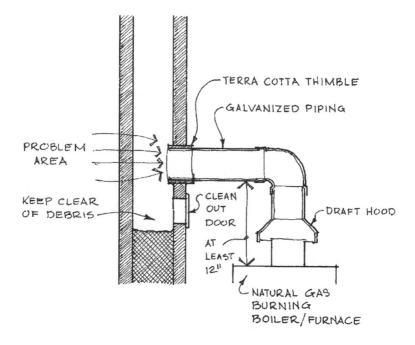

TERRA COTTA THIMBLE

GALVANIZED PIPING

PROBLEM AREA

KEEP CLEAR OF DEBRIS

CLEAN OUT DOOR

DRAFT HOOD

AT LEAST 12"

NATURAL GAS BURNING BOILER/FURNACE

BLOCKED CHIMNEY

FIGURE 55

I was once called on a job because paint kept blistering on the chimney wall on the floor above the gas boiler. I immediately suspected that the flue for the boiler was partly blocked and that some of the steam, one of byproducts of burning natural gas, was condensing in the flue and then leaking through the wall. What I found was a *completely blocked* flue—I removed two 5-gallon buckets of sopping wet flue liner shards, which had fallen down from the deteriorating chimney top. The wonder was that all the inhabitants of the house were not dead. The difference, I believe, was that both parents went elsewhere to work every day and all the kids were in school. After school and on weekends, this house was a veritable mecca for all the neighborhood kids, everyone coming and going all day and into the night, the front and back doors opening and closing non-stop. In addition, it was a leaky old house. Summertime only saw carbon monoxide from the hot water heater, which was also completely blocked.

They'd had the problem of peeling paint for many years and had repaired and repainted this wall several times. They had believed that rain was coming down from the top of the chimney despite a rain cap.

The other potentially serious carbon monoxide problem I have first-hand knowledge of happened partly on my watch. I'd actually created the problem. A young man named Joe was renting a big, broken-down house near DuPont Circle in downtown Washington. His two great loves were the house's fireplace and his dog. But the fireplace smoked badly, for a number of reasons. He also had a terrible chimney for his old boiler, which was on the second floor. It was too small and protruded above the roof only about a foot, among other things, and it was made out of cast iron sewer pipe, a definite code violation on several scores.

Anyway, Joe was on a tight budget and said he could only afford to fix the fireplace, which I did. (His landlord wouldn't pay for anything, the usual pattern in Washington.) A couple of weeks later I called him to find out if everything was working to his satisfaction. He bragged to me about how much he was now able to use his fireplace.

A couple of months later I bumped into him on the street. He looked awful. He said he'd just got out of the hospital where he'd been treated for carbon monoxide poisoning. What had happened is that his continuous use of the fireplace had drained his house of so much air that the inadequate boiler chimney simply would not draw and instead filled his house with carbon monoxide. If the boiler had been in the basement—there was no basement—or on the first floor, I think it would have been far less dangerous. To think I had almost been involved, if only indirectly, in killing someone! I've always wondered about his dog. Isn't carbon monoxide heavier than air? Lying on the floor could have been very dangerous.

I consider this similar to "my cowboy" lighting his house on fire, which I described in Chapter I. They were both "extreme events", conceivable, really bad things that could happen but almost never do, a Black Swan event. In each case, imprudent, extreme action was taken because of what I said or did, the former just once, the latter over several months. To some extent I was the enabler.

Of the thousands of fireplaces I have inspected, 2 of the heavily used ones with gas logs had closed dampers. The homeowners never opened them. They were living their lives as if nothing was wrong. They seemed healthy. They were not even pale or depressed. I was amazed.

My view of deaths by carbon monoxide poisoning is that it's not easy to make it happen even under the most threatening conditions! There are certainly lots of sicknesses caused by carbon monoxide, which do not lead to death. These sicknesses are never accurately diagnosed or documented.

SWITCHING A FIREPLACE FROM WOOD TO NATURAL GAS

I have been told many times by frustrated owners of smoking fireplaces that they've decided to switch to gas logs. I always advise them to think this decision through carefully. If the fireplace you are burning wood in smokes, it will almost certainly also leak the byproducts of burning natural gas, one of which is carbon monoxide, which is toxic and colorless and without odor. At least with wood as the fuel you can see and smell what's leaking.

A possibly wiser choice, I advise them, if they don't care to address the smoking problem is ventless gas logs whose byproducts are carbon *dioxide*, which is a non-toxic substance, and water vapor. These ventless gas logs have been designed to burn the natural gas completely. While the flames are less dramatic than regular gas logs, ventless logs are also more energy efficient because *all the heat* from combustion stays in the house as the chimney is sealed shut.

What concerns me here is that the fireplace will be switched to regular gas logs without anyone fixing the smoking problem. If only half the carbon monoxide still remains in the house, this scenario is still not in the interest of the best health. Have you ever heard of a doctor inquiring about where you live, your living conditions? The potential dangers of your home? Yet the natural gas retailers promote switching fuels from wood to gas as if there were no possible risk. Even the ventless gas logs make me a little nervous. Do they really work 100% reliably? (I think it's rare that any machine is 100% reliable.) Some states and jurisdictions have banned ventless gas fireplaces. Whatever kind of gas fireplace you select, I recommend installing a good carbon monoxide detector nearby.

CANDLES

Another statistic: from 2004 to 2011 candles in the home started fires which killed more than 1,000 people and injured many thousands more. Candles—big, long-burning candles, not regular ones you put on a birthday cake or the dinner table—are therefore much more dangerous than fireplaces! Who would have thought that possible? *Candles are so dangerous because no one takes them seriously.* How about bathtubs? Every year over 1,000 elderly people are killed or seriously injured in bathtub accidents. More than 100 babies drown in bathtubs every year. People die from dog bites, skiing accidents, and hoodie drawstrings. How could fireplaces be so darned safe? One of the reasons they are so safe is that they are specially-designed and specially-built machines for burning wood in a specially-designated area. Fireplaces are built to comply with strict codes and generally do. The other reason is because most of us, when using our fireplaces, normally exercise considerable caution, an attitude I strongly approve of.

The main point about chimney fires—fires where creosote is burning inside the chimney—is not their danger but their drama: to the uninitiated, a really big chimney fire is absolutely

terrifying. The chimney has become a blast furnace. It is sucking
so hard, it's like having a huge commercial jet plane in your living
room. Every possible aperture to the outside is vibrating and
whistling, trying to restore air pressure inside the house. It is
very noisy, very unnerving. But, in almost all cases, the properly-
built masonry chimney holds up fine—confines the fire inside
the flue—and doesn't set the house on fire. Moreover, the house
doesn't quite collapse because tons of house air has been sucked
up the chimney! There's still enough oxygen to support life!

More seriously, most fireplace chimney fires are extremely
brief—under four minutes—and frequently not even noticed
by the homeowner unless there is a very, very significant
build-up of creosote. The racket of the chimney fire is typically
drowned out by the TV. When my wife and I would take evening
walks in Washington, DC, we would sometimes see dark smoke
billowing out a chimney top. This was not normal smoke from
a wood fire. It was a *chimney fire smoke*, pure and simple. Once
you've smelled chimney fire smoke, you never forget it. But the
owners of the house were oblivious—we could see them eating
and talking, walking around—because it was so brief and so
completely contained. On the other hand, *wood stove chimney
fires*, especially air-tight stoves hooked up to a masonry chimney
without a metal sleeve lining the flue all the way to the top,
are intrinsically dangerous because so much more creosote is
produced. This kind of chimney fire can burn for hours. Most
jurisdictions now outlaw such potentially dangerous hook-ups.
It is made far worse by the use of bad wood.

For the record, even this kind of chimney fire almost never lights
the house on fire.

What happens in a fireplace chimney fire depends on the amount
of creosote and the design of the fireplace. If a fireplace has
no smoke shelf, burning creosote can fall through the damper
opening, into the firebox and beyond, if there happens to be lots
and lots of creosote. The chimney fire I have in mind occurred
with a Rumford fireplace where uncured, oversized logs had

been burned for a couple of seasons—2 to 3 cords—and, then the next season, well cured, 3-inch logs were burned, which started a big chimney fire. Had the damper been all the way forward— the technically better position for ordinary fireplaces—and had the fireplace included a spacious smoke shelf, most of the burning creosote would have ended up on the smoke shelf and never made it down to the firebox. In this unusual case, however, lots of the burning creosote ended up beyond the outer hearth, pock-marking the wood floor. No one was hurt and the only damage was what I call floor stigmata. I consider this chimney fire another one of those "extreme events," rare but illustrative on how things can sometimes go surprisingly wrong. My advice: don't burn poor wood and, if you do—many of us do just out of sheer stubbornness, we want to use it up—make sure to have your chimney swept before burning good wood. Good wood burns much hotter than bad wood and has a much longer flame.

NFPA's 2013 report only mentions fireplaces in the following statement: "Fireplaces, chimneys or chimney connectors were involved in two of every five (39%) of reported home heating fires in 2007-2011. Failure to clean was a factor in roughly three out of five (57%) such incidents." The important point is that no property damage and no harm was done, especially, no deaths. If there had been deaths, NFPA would have said so. The chimney connectors mentioned above are the piping from wood stoves to a chimney. Fireplace chimney fires inside the chimney, I believe, are remarkably harmless.

THIRD DEGREE CREOSOTE
This is the hard, shiny, black stuff created by running an airtight stove with little or no air/oxygen. It simply cannot be swept out of a chimney using regular sweeping technology. There are 3 alternative strategies. The first is to use the fireplaces, adding chemical compounds to the fire, which are supposed to loosen the creosote enough so it can be swept out. This is the only strategy I have ever used and it worked moderately well. It wasn't particularly expensive. I never did it when there was more than ¼" of 3rd degree creosote. The second is to use a liquid, which dissolves the creosote.

This requires special spraying equipment and I understand is messy. It works but is not cheap and may have to be done more than once. The third strategy is to break it up by lighting it on fire. This is immediately followed by sweeping. Again, special equipment is needed for this and know-how. I have seen it done once. The key is to be able to control the burn by judiciously restricting the throat damper.

FIREPLACE HEARTH FIRES

Fires starting in the *proximity* of the firebox of a fireplace are a much more serious threat than chimney fires. The 2012 NFPA report attributes six deaths to fires starting in the "Crawl space or substructure space." See Figure 56.

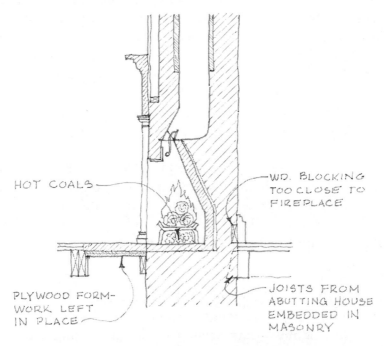

HOT COALS

WD. BLOCKING TOO CLOSE TO FIREPLACE

PLYWOOD FORM-WORK LEFT IN PLACE

JOISTS FROM ABUTTING HOUSE EMBEDDED IN MASONRY

COMBUSTIBLES TOO NEAR FIREBOX

FIGURE 56

The scenario that I fear the most is one where a fireplace has been used for many years in fires *of relatively short duration—* three hours or less—and is therefore considered "safe." And then that fireplace is cranked up for eight hours or more.

Two of the most serious fireplace fires I was called upon to evaluate after the fact were caused by college students pulling all-nighters as they prepared for final exams. They kept a big fire going for many, many hours. The heat from the ever-growing bed of hot coals finally reached combustibles, in one case the wooden baseboard nailer in the row house next door and, in another, the wood underneath the inner hearth. A surprising number of old fireplaces have these defects, maybe as many as fifteen per cent.

What makes this scenario so dangerous is that it can even happen *after the fire has died down* and the operator is no longer in attendance, having finally retired. The large bed of coals keeps radiating lots of heat, which continues to slowly migrate, eventually reaching wood. Because the chimney is still warm and the damper still open, the first 10-20 minutes of smoke from burning joists, nailers, baseboards, etc. is whisked away up the chimney and does not get a chance to set off the smoke alarms. By the time they do blow, the fire has really spread.

For the record, fire inspectors don't always understand how dangerous a fire of long duration can be. In one of the cases I was involved in, when a fire of many hours had finally ignited a joist, the inspector called it an electrical fire just because there happened to be some charred wires nearby. I'm almost sure it wasn't.

Voltaire writes to a friend in 1724 how the house he was living in was set on fire by a wooden beam *under the front hearth of the fireplace.* Many a time, when rebuilding existing fireplaces, I've found charred wood members under the front hearth. We've been struggling with this particular problem for literally hundreds of years.

THE FIREPLACE SAFETY INSPECTION

The first thing I do is go to the basement. If it's unfinished, you can look between the joists right under the front hearth and see how it's constructed. Typically, the joists have been headed off and a wood form is still there holding a concrete pad. Right below the front of the fireplace opening, there should be at least five inches of masonry between the front edge of the front firebox firebrick and the wood below. Usually this concrete slab angles up as it goes in to the room—becomes less deep—and attaches to the doubled joist header. Other times, it's a rectangular box, all the same depth.

In houses built 100 years ago, the inner and outer hearth of the fireplace is often supported by a shallow brick arch. Often the wood support used to construct the arch is still there. This must be removed. If the outer hearth alone is supported by a shallow brick arch—it often has become unstable in addition to still having its inadequate temporary wood lathe support system—it usually needs to be replaced with a thicker, poured, reinforced concrete base.

If the basement is finished so I can't see, I first check the outer hearth in front of the fireplace. If it looks like the hearthstone or tile might have been laid directly on the wood floor, I drill a hole in the mortar joint between the front hearth and the inner hearth using a small masonry bit. I angle the bit into the house, not into the fireplace. If the outer hearth is sitting on wood, I will hit wood in an inch or so. (Obviously, if the hearth has shifted, cracked or is unstable, it needs to be redone in any case.) If there is no problem—if I never hit wood after drilling several inches—I just fill in the little hole I've made with new mortar.

The kind of hearth that draws my attention is raised and inch or slightly less from the floor. Sometimes, by knocking on the hearthstone you can determine if it's solid masonry underneath or more or less just sitting on wood. It makes a certain kind of hollow sound on wood. If the stone or tile hearth is flush with the floor, it is more likely that it was built to code. If I'm suspicious, which I often am, I have to make one or more holes in the finished drywall ceiling in the basement below to determine without a doubt that there are no combustibles near by.

To determine if there is wood behind the back wall of the firebox almost always requires that you remove one or more courses of firebrick. After removing any wood you find, you then rebuild, adding high temperature insulating board or insulating brick. If it's a row house, I also may have to remove some of the back hearth bricks and dig down to establish that there is no joist end from the adjoining house. In single detached homes, I've encountered almost no mistakes. Obviously, if the fireplace is on an exterior wall, the usual location for the last 60 years, there's almost never this kind of safety problem.

There may be a problem, however, with heat loss if the back wall of the fireplace is not insulated with a high temperature material. (I once had a very observant and conscientious homeowner call to ask if the outside brick wall of an exterior fireplace, which became hot during her fires, posed any risk! The outside wall was in her back yard. It didn't and doesn't.)

A sticky problem with chimneys is that there is not supposed to be any combustibles in direct contact with the outside of a chimney. The various codes aren't in agreement on this issue. The Canadian code calls for 2" between the outside of a chimney and wood. Sheet metal or flashing could be used on exterior chimneys where they abut the house. Inside the house, sheet rock is allowed but not insulation, which would trap heat. Interestingly enough, the corners of the chimneys are seen as less likely to transfer heat to combustibles. (I speculate that the corners of flue liners are always rounded and that heat to the outside corner of the brick would have to travel at least 20% farther than straight through the brick.) American codes are less strict, 2" for interior chimneys and 1" for exterior. The reason this issue is so sticky is because a great many chimneys do not comply with even the most lax code. What I hope to find is a well-lined chimney with at least some kind of air space between the liner and the inside of the chimney brick, not easily determined. But I also look out for wood members—joists, rafters, flooring or trim—actually touching the chimney. These should be removed. The key is that there is free movement of air between the chimney and any combustible. An even more serious problem is when wood, i.e., a rafter, is actually embedded into the chimney.

(This failing—wood touching the outside of a chimney—is most likely with chimneys more than a hundred years old.)

A further complication in making this safety inspection is that often the chimney is enclosed where you need to determine there are the appropriate clearances. I believe that a means of monitoring should be available. I start to get concerned when temperatures of the outside of the brick are greater than 100 degrees F., extremely rare in my experience. All woods don't ignite at the same temperature. Two hundred degrees indicates real danger as far as I'm concerned. Soft woods like pine and hemlock will ignite at lower temperatures than hard woods like oak. This is because they contain resins. Most wood used today in framing a house is soft wood.

It's important to note that today's codes are based on confining the heat from a big chimney fire of long duration, not the heat from ordinary use.

SUMMARY OF RISKS

To summarize risk factors, in order of importance:

- Combustibles too near under the front hearth, anywhere under the inner hearth, or behind the back wall. This becomes a problem with *long* fires, which create a large bed of red-hot coals, which will continue to radiate heat long after regular combustion has ended. *Long duration of fire, anything longer than 4 hours,* thus becomes a very real risk factor. The longer the fire, the greater the risk.

- Combustibles like furniture, firewood, rugs, etc. within 4 feet of an open fire. (Maybe even farther away with a really hot fire.)
- Lack of attention to keeping all fuel and hot coals completely inside the firebox. Wood for refueling should not be anywhere near where it could be ignited by radiant heat from the firebox.
- No screen in front of the fireplace to stop flying sparks when you're not in full attendance.
- Use of inappropriate substances, especially liquids, to start the fire like gasoline, diesel oil, kerosene, etc. (I once worked on a fireplace where the man of the house routinely used tubes of construction glue as kindling! He said they burned great. They do but his wife and I agreed that this was crazy.)
- Another more awkward risk is children. They want to help, i.e., throw the logs on the blistering fire. Some young kids at certain times and ages are flighty and super casual, super cool. The idea of caution is beneath them. It's not hip. One way around this is to engage them in laying the fire in the first place, when there's no heat and zero risk. You would then stress that it's your job to rearrange the logs and feed the fire once it's going because it's too darned dangerous. Don't give in on this! Age 12 might be a good time to let them start practicing, under your watchful eye. My greatest fears regarding kids and fire is that a little girl with a fancy, flammable nightgown could incinerate herself. No one should ever play, rough house, or fool around within 8 feet of a roaring fire!
- Failure to have the chimney swept. (I recommend sweeping every four to five cords of wood or more frequently if bad wood has been burned or if there is a noticeable buildup of creosote in the first few flue liners, ¾ inch all the way around.)

The interesting pattern here is that the first factor mentioned above—combustibles near the inner hearth or behind the back wall—is a failure on the part of the way the fireplace was built.

All the other failures are *operator* failures or errors, i.e., not exercising judgment, not paying attention, not showing patience starting a fire, not being vigilant about kids, etc.

To follow up on what I said about smoking: it's almost never the homeowner's fault. It's the fault of the architect and/or the fireplace builder. (It is true, however, that a skilled fireplace operator can often make a terrible fireplace work.) With safety, on the other hand, as I just explained, it's usually the fault of the homeowner. The exception is the unexpected (and completely unpublicized) danger with *fires of long duration,* where fault must be laid at the door of the fireplace builder.

For the record, it has been my impression that at least 50 years must elapse before fireplace design and construction mistakes are identified and rectified. In other words, the architects and workmen have left for the great unknown believing they had designed and built great fireplaces. I suppose this is also true in other spheres of life. We human beings are almost never found out! We almost never pay the price for our unintentional misdeeds!

Other fireplace-related fires I was called to investigate actually had nothing to do with the fireplace. Three of them related to ash pits, which many fireplaces have underneath their hearths and serve as a convenient place to dispose of ashes. In one instance, a fire in the exposed metal piping to the ash pit set the whole house on fire, another example of an "extreme event", something that could conceivably happens but almost never does. Normally, you don't have piping but a chute and ash pit, both completely enclosed in masonry. What happens in these worst cases is that unburned wood still on the hearth from previous fires is swept into the ash pit. And then, at another time, a live coal is mistakenly swept into the ash pit and lights the unburned pieces of wood. If there's enough unburned pieces of wood, it can smolder for weeks.

If I'm doing other work on a fireplace, I press the homeowner to let me remove the ash pit door and brick up the opening in the hearth. I must have done this 100 times. It's fairly straightforward. The door itself is often brick size. But right below it are often ledges. I usually end up using Portland and sand for the mortar. Sometimes, I've had to insert a piece of rebar to hold up the brick. See Figure 57.

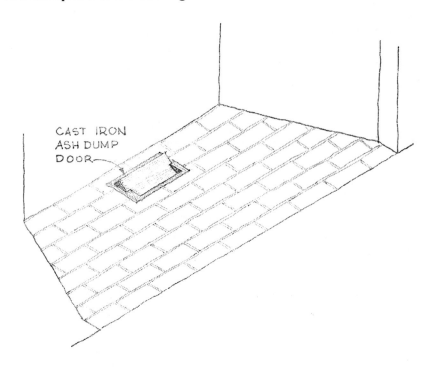

FIREPLACE ASH DUMP DOOR
FIGURE 57

When I have been called to inspect after a major chimney fire showed me just how clean an old chimney could become! The prefab chimneys looked brand new, spanking clean. The terra cotta lined chimneys had some hairline cracking near the top but were completely stable. All traces of creosote were gone. But, as

I've mentioned, frequent big chimney fires simply can't be good for any chimney system.

With wood stoves, a similar practice, on a small scale, should be done intentionally on a daily basis: get a really hot fire going to flush out the system, not restricting the air supply to the stove at all. Of course, this assumes you have a correctly installed, tight, closed system, which would include a metal pipe from the stove to the chimney top, installed inside a masonry chimney. Preferably, the pipe would be insulated, especially where winters are severe. (Factory-made insulated chimneys are also available.) Frequent mini-chimney fires insure the safest operation of any serious woodstove system.

Summary

Fireplaces are remarkably safe. Other human activities including cooking and bathing are much more dangerous. Death by carbon monoxide poisoning, despite extensive regulation, is much more likely. Fireplace chimney fires are in fact rare, rarely reported to the authorities, and rarely serious. Fireplace hearth fires are more likely and much more serious. Duration of a regular fire is a risk factor in hearth fires. Ash pit fires. The fireplace safety inspection.

CHAPTER VII

FIREWOOD

CONTENTS

Firewood with sap in it won't burn well—Trees should be cut when the sap is in the roots—Problem with solid fuels—Burning wood is environmentally OK—Buying wood

To repeat what I said earlier about firewood: What determines good firewood is *when* the tree was cut down. If it was cut when the sap was up, it will take far longer to cure and, with some kinds of wood, curing never seems to occur.

Professional firewood suppliers do all their felling of trees in the dead of winter. Later, they go back, haul the logs out of the forest, and finally cut them up and split them. The wood then cures for at least six months before being sold and burned. If not sold that year, it's sold early the next.

If a *tree surgeon group* tries to sell you wood from a tree they've just cut down, and it's spring or summer, it's a certainty that there is lots of sap in the wood and will require at least another year to cure before it will burn. (A standing dead elm, i.e., dead for years, is the exception. It burns great.) It's been my experience that wood from oak trees never cures properly if cut when its sap is up.

I think tree sellers justify flogging bad wood on customers because they imagine that it will eventually become usable. In many locales, tree men double as the main purveyors of firewood. This can cause no end of mischief.

Wood that's fit to burn is usually split into pieces no thicker than three to four inches. It lights readily. It does not just char. Steam or sap does not pour out the ends of the logs as they try to burn. When you add a new log to the fire's bed of coals, it ignites almost immediately. Where the manufacture of wood pellets for pellet stoves was a real advance in wood burning is that it increased the surface area available for burning. Additionally, the fuel was more like a liquid because it could be poured.

The flaw with wood in its natural state—as logs—is the same flaw we see with any solid fuel, most of it can't burn because it's protected by its outside wood. The result is that much of the fuel is heated just enough to become a gas but not enough to take the important step of ignition and burning. An unburned gas, smoke, is what causes creosote or, in the case of coal, soot, and is a serious atmospheric pollutant.

The difficulty with burning a solid is typically at the beginning of a fire, when the fire is not hot enough or large enough. It is at this point that fire lighting squares are so effective: they light immediately and immediately put out lots of heat.

One way to determine if wood is cured is by smell. Green oak has a pronounced sour/sweet smell. It doesn't seem to make any difference if the ends of the logs have cracks. It helps if the bark is loose or falling off but the only certain test for cured wood is trying to burn it. A moisture gauge used by painters is useless because it only tells the moisture percentage on the outside of a piece of wood. Burnable firewood has 15% or less moisture content.

WAX LOGS NOT RECOMMENDED
Sometimes homeowners retreat to those fake logs you can buy
at the supermarket, mainly for their convenience. They burn for
about an hour. They give off slightly less smoke than firewood plus
a fair amount of heat. They also have almost no start-up phase,
the time in the cycle of fireplace use where smoking is most likely
and worst.

The disadvantages of fake logs are that any smoking that
does occur will stain much more than wood smoke and more
permanently. (To me, the smoke is much more caustic than wood
smoke.) But, even worse, burning these logs leaves a waxy residue
inside the firebox and chimney, making sweeping much nastier.
Normal creosote is flakey and dry, some of it slightly coarse. It
may stain your skin a little, especially if you are sweating, but it
won't stick to your drop cloths, your tools, your person, especially
your skin, like super glue. Its worst problem is how fine—how
small its feathery particles of residue are. I have turned down
sweeping and repair jobs where people have been burning those
darned logs. The only remedy for the condition is long, hot, fires
burning seasoned wood. You must get the fireplace and chimney
really hot for several hours on numerous occasions.

BURNING WOOD IS ENVIRONMENTALLY OK

My favorite wood book is "Heating With Wood" by Larry Gay. He
writes, "The single, most important fact about the products of
combustion of wood is that these would be liberated in the forest
by decay anyway and do not, therefore, lead to a net increase in
environmental pollution." (Page 17) Unlike coal, wood contains
no sulfur and no heavy metals. Why this is I'm not sure. Don't
they both come from the same thing: decaying plant matter?
The environmental problems with wood burning are almost
completely caused by *incomplete* combustion, especially in areas
like Boulder, which is located in a geographic bowl. Of course,
the *scale* of the burning of Amazonian rain forests is obviously
extremely serious. And some people are allergic to wood smoke.

To minimize the amount of pollution thrown into the air, have long, hot fires, which *consume* all the smoke. Smoldering fires are a true abomination: no heat and lots of particulate pollution. Hint: proper restriction of the top damper virtually eliminates air pollution. If the chimney flue temperature is greater than 300 degrees, all particulates (smoke) and other byproducts are completely burned up. The biggest problem with fireplace use is the start-up before the higher temperatures are reached. I think start-up should be less than 5 minutes. Lots of 1-inch fuel, along with a good fire starter, is a must for this phase.

My environmental justification for the use of wood is to reduce fossil fuel use for central heating. Trees that are used for firewood do not generally have other uses, at least in the United States and Canada. I'm thinking especially of the hardwoods. For example, the amount of oak used in flooring, furniture, veneer, construction planking, etc. probably constitutes less than 40% of the total oak available. Prime oak logs sell at a premium to industries that can use them. The rest of these trees are more or less ignored.

Increasing the efficiencies of our fireplaces is important if we are trying to reduce our carbon footprint. Masonry and rocket stoves also burn wood much more completely than regular wood stoves or fireplaces and extract far more useable heat from the wood. I believe these highly efficient stoves will become much more popular in years to come. To locate masonry stove builders in your area, look up www.mha-net.org. For information on Rocket Stoves....

I don't want to minimize the role of trees in storing carbon dioxide. I'm assuming that old trees cut for firewood will soon be replaced by newer, faster-growing trees. Trees grow fastest from a height of 25' to 75', perhaps from 8 years to 20. Mature trees grow much more slowly.

VARIETIES OF WOOD

All woods burn differently. Any of the fir family of trees burns with a longer flame, presumably because of their resins. Hard woods, which are denser, burn more slowly than soft woods. I know a man who only burns apple wood because he likes the color of the flames. Fruitwoods generally have especially beautiful flames. Driftwood has a very blue flame, I assume because of the salt in the wood. Black locust burns very hot. Each wood, I've noticed, leaves a different quality of ash. When an ash wood burns, it leaves an ash ghost of its former self. Each wood also makes a slightly different noise or vibration as it burns.

Gay, the author of <u>Heating With Wood</u>, includes a wonderful anonymous poem, the second stanza of which reads as follows:

> Birch and fir logs burn too fast,
> Blaze up bright and do not last.
> It is by the Irish said
> Hawthorne bakes the sweetest bread.
> Elm wood burns like churchyard mold,
> E'en the very flames are cold.
> But ash green or ash brown
> Is fit for queen with golden crown.

This poem strongly conveys that different woods burn differently. I was not aware that green ash would burn well and am still not completely convinced. If it is possible, it is probably because it was burned right after being cut down in mid-winter.

The key guide to choosing the right wood is what's locally available, what most people are using, and, obviously, price. A key piece of information is how well it burns, which, as I've said, is determined by when it was cut down. It should also cure for some months after being split.

WOODS THAT MAKE FLYING SPARKS

Two of the woods that make flying sparks are hemlock and, believe it or not, poplar. (I read that larch is another offender.) The sparks are made by pockets of air in the body of the wood fibers. As these air pockets are heated, they can explode. I suspect that other woods also have air pockets but not in such abundance. Whenever you absent yourself from a burning fire, you should put a screen in front of it in the event that an air pocket in the wood explodes.

BUYING WOOD

Another issue is how to buy wood. I've already pointed out that most wood cut when the sap was up won't burn very well. I've had two customers who insisted on burning wood that had been cut down at the wrong time of year. Both ended up having enormous chimney fires despite frequent chimney sweeping. In one case, their wood supplier was actually in the firewood business and still did not understand the importance of only felling his product when its sap was in the roots.

In the Washington metropolitan area, a lot of firewood is hawked virtually door to door on pickup trucks. It is not sold by the cord but by the "rick", which turns out to be about a third of a cord. If possible, it's in the wood burner's interest to buy firewood by the cord, which is an established measure by volume, 4 feet wide, 4 feet tall and 8 feet long or 128 cubic feet. It weighs roughly two tons. A cord of wood cannot be hauled around on a ½ ton pick-up truck! Or even a 1-ton pick-up.

If you burn significantly less than a cord a year or don't have space for a full cord, buy a half cord, called a face cord in the business. Sometimes you can split a cord with a neighbor.

The economics of hawking firewood in metropolitan Washington (and probably other metropolitan areas) suggest that better deals may be possible at the *end of the day*, if you're buying from someone who knocks on your door. A significant percentage of the wood hawker's expense is delivering it. They probably do not want to haul it back home 20-50 miles away. They may be willing to deal.

When I first arrived in Washington, DC in the late '70's, the quality of the firewood hawked door to door was not reliable. Sometimes it was good, sometimes not. By the time I left 40 years later, the quality was uniformly superb.

Buying at the end of the heating season can be a problem because the wood may have been cut down and split only a month or two before and hasn't had much time to cure.

The other issue is wood storage. I think it's criminal not to store firewood under cover, even if the cover is modest, like a piece of metal roofing or even an old piece of plywood. I also like it to be off the ground. Even good wood burns less well if it has just been snowed or rained on. What happens has two bad effects: because of the extra water, heat has to be used to make steam before the wood will burn. The other bad effect is that there is more creosote deposition of the kind that simply cannot be removed with normal sweeping.

It probably makes sense not to buy more wood than you would normally use in a year or two, unless you're storing it in a completely dry place.

SUMMARY

Firewood should contain 15% or less moisture. Uncured firewood will not burn completely and pollutes the atmosphere. What determines good firewood is determined by when it was cut down. Don't use fake logs! Burning wood is environmentally OK. In fact, you should be able to decrease your carbon footprint by burning wood. Buying wood.

CHAPTER VIII

RACCOONS IN FIREPLACE CHIMNEYS

CONTENTS

Raccoons are the only animal I know of that can negotiate a vertical tube like a chimney—They especially like fireplace chimneys—They don't like the smell of chimneys that have been used for wood burning—Eviction strategies—How smart raccoons are

One of my most surprising discoveries when I began sweeping chimneys in the late 1970's was that raccoons actually *seek out* chimneys to live in. Or at least that's what I first thought. I've now refined that idea: they seek out just the *right kind of fireplace chimneys,* mainly to give birth and raise their young but also as second and third homes. The key feature that raccoons seek is a spacious, dry smoke shelf. See Figure 58.

RACCOONS IN THE
CHIMNEY

FIGURE 58

What makes it so perfect is its design, which serves as a free baby-sitter, because the raccoon pups are too small to climb up out of the chimney unassisted. It's one hundred per cent safe from canine predators like dogs. It's also usually dry all the time, unlike the other possible nursery, the storm sewer. The astonishing thing is that raccoons ever figured this out in the first place.

If you ever hear a chirping sound on the smoke shelf of an unused fireplace, it's probably not the sound of a bird singing at the top of your chimney, the sound being carried down the chimney ever so clearly. It's a family of baby raccoons within a couple feet of you, babbling away on your smoke shelf.

If your dog suddenly becomes very interested in a fireplace, you have raccoons on the smoke shelf. He/she can smell them.

If you start finding fleas in front of the fireplace or you start smelling a sharp gamey odor, it can't be anything else.

The key point here is that you *never use* that fireplace! *No self-respecting animal dwells in a chimney that's being used for burning wood. He won't even scout it out. As I've mentioned before, if it stinks a little to us, it really, really stinks to any animal. Their noses are much better than ours, maybe 100 times better.*

Sweeping does not remove this creosote stink. In fact, it may increase it because it may expose a fresher layer of old creosote. (This is another reason to increase the air pressure in the house if you have a low chimney: if you don't, it will always smell around the fireplace, even with the damper closed.)

But raccoons also dwell in chimneys when they're not raising their young. My theory is that each raccoon has several chimneys it calls home.

This was suggested to me by what happened to a customer. He called to report that, one evening while he was sitting in his living room reading a book, something had urinated down his chimney. First he heard the falling water noise and then there was the powerful urine smell. What animal could this be and what could be done, he wanted to know? I advised him to use the fireplace as if his life depended on it. Not only would long hot fires consume the urine smell but they would inoculate the chimney against further invasions. The raccoon was simply laying claim to this particular chimney, probably because he smelled that another raccoon had been there. After the raccoon(s) were all surely long gone, having been routed by the smell of creosote, I'd come back and put a screen on the top of the chimney as a permanent barrier to further intrusions.

OTHER EVICTION STRATEGIES

There are other ways to evict raccoons, with which I have had mixed success. One is to force them, using noise, to leave, which works if it's only adults. You bang on the damper, set up the radio in the fireplace playing real loud rock music, heavy metal, etc. (I never did use RAP.)

I once lit a fire in the fireplace to drive out a raccoon. He wouldn't leave right away but when he did, he stuck only his head out of the chimney and rested for a couple of minutes, panting. When he then moved completely out of the chimney, I could see that lots of his fur was singed and still smoking. I never tried that again!

MOTHBALLS

Another strategy is to throw mothballs onto the smoke shelf and then close the damper. After a few days, put on a good screen. I did this a couple of times with success. Then one time I asked the homeowner to do the mothball part. I in turn put on the screen after a couple of days, but without being able to get into the house to check that Mr. Raccoon had indeed left. Well, the poor guy got trapped in the chimney, died and began to rot, making a very big stink, which I then had to deal with. What had happened is the homeowner *failed to close* the damper all the way, so the chimney draft carried away the fumes from the mothballs. Mr. Raccoon had no good reason to leave. When I inspected my screen, it had blood on it. He probably died of dehydration. I had to cut into the chimney from the outside at the smoke shelf level to get him out. Did I feel stupid!

For the record, the mothball trick only works when the damper closes very tightly. I had checked out this particular damper! It shut perfectly. Lesson: never trust someone to do something who is not *intimately familiar* with the machinery and dynamic involved. Even the well-intentioned can make big mistakes.

THE POWER OF THE BARK

One of my chimney associates in the old days, Jim Schule, would take very dramatic action: He would get as near as he could to the raccoon and then, out of the blue and without warning the homeowner, he'd begin to growl and howl and bark like there was no tomorrow. It was astonishingly convincing and effective. Even though raccoons are nocturnal creatures, they would vacate the chimney premises almost immediately into the full light of day. Homeowners were very impressed.

Another strategy is to drive the raccoon out with your chimney sweeping brush. I'd had a number of successes with this technique. But once when I was also able to persuade/help the young raccoons up the flue, it turned disastrous. Only the mother survived. The little ones were simply too small and inexperienced to climb down from the tall chimney top without falling. It was made worse by them not dying instantly when they hit the ground and requiring me to put them out of their misery. Yuk! It was this event that persuaded me the animal rescue people should be called unless it was only adult raccoons and very straight-forward. *The most economical and humane strategy for the homeowner remains to use your fireplace.* No raccoon will enter a chimney flue that's been used for burning lots of wood within the last year. It simply smells too awful.

THE FASHION STATEMENT

An earlier time when I used my brush to evict an adult raccoon, I thought I'd succeeded only to find that it had *come back through my brush* and was lying calmly in a fashion statement on the granite kitchen counter, its tail artfully drooping over the edge. It was clear to me that it had been inside peoples' houses before and had closely observed the décor. I was able to persuade her (Today, after some reflection, I'm almost certain it was a her!) to leave by the nearby back door.

Another earlier time, my brother Nick, who worked with me one sweeping season, used persuasion alone. He somehow *talked a family of raccoons*—mother and three babies—into climbing down off the smoke shelf into the living room and walking calmly out the back door. It took Nick forty minutes. If I had not witnessed this, I would not have believed it. Who needs St. Francis of Assisi when you have Nick?

Again, I doubt very much if the mother raccoon was not familiar with the layout of the inside of the house. She had checked it out, probably helping herself to the occasional snack but very judiciously. As you can see, I believe raccoons know us humans pretty well.

HOME TURF

One of my first raccoon experiences ended in a tussle on top of the chimney. I had forced him out of the chimney with my brush but he was damned if he was leaving. See Figure 59.

HOME TURF

FIGURE 59

This was *his* chimney, damn it. I was standing on a ladder. I never saw him whack/bite me but the back of my left hand suddenly hurt like crazy and very soon began to swell up. I assumed he was not rabid, I guess, because he was just defending his home turf. I got a tetanus booster shot instead of the rabies shots. But it continued to swell and hurt. I even lanced it. Finally, one of my sweep associates, Bill Smith, asked me if I'd ever tried Epsom salts. In fact, I had tried soaking my hand in an Epsom salt solution. But what Bill meant was *drinking* a solution of Epsom salts—a half teaspoon dissolved in half a glass of warm water. I did that and within 30 seconds the wound opened up like a flower and pus poured forth. After a few minutes, it closed up again, tight as a drum. I did this twice a day for a week, it continuing to work but less dramatically as the swelling went down. I've since learned that drinking an Epsom salt solution is an old-timey hillbilly cure for boils. (Epsom salts are made of magnesium sulfate.) Doctors I've told this tale to just roll their eyes.

To me the extraordinary thing about raccoons is how smart they are. Compared to other animals that end up in chimneys, like squirrels or birds, raccoons are geniuses. In addition to discovering chimneys at all, raccoons negotiate chimneys the way the famous climbing boys or sweeps of the 18th and 19th centuries did: they almost certainly press outwards with their limbs. (The sweeps famously used their elbows and knees, which I'm assuming raccoons also do.) The other way they show smarts is staying calm in a completely new situation. Lying on a kitchen countertop, pretending you're supposed to be there, shows real imagination. Being willing to do what my brother Nick was coaxing you to do is also impressive. Just try and catch a squirrel acting in such an inspired way!

It's interesting how homeowners react when I tell them they have a family of raccoons in their house. Most of them say to let them be and to come back to screen the top in a few months time, when the babies have grown up and left.

The squirrels I have found in chimneys were dead, as were the birds. They fell in and couldn't get out. Squirrels and birds don't intentionally go down a chimney; they fall in. I suppose a hummingbird could fly down a chimney (and out again) if it wanted to. Maybe bats? I think chimney swift is a misnomer. Normal birds cannot negotiate a vertical shaft.

RACCOONS AS MEMBERS OF THE BEAR FAMILY

Once I found several birds on the smoke shelf of a fireplace along with lots of egg shells. What was happening—and had happened for years—was probably as follows. There was a break in the piece of flue liner perhaps 3 inches below the chimney top, which made a perfect nook for a bird's nest. (I saw that it had been used for that.) It was accessible by air and sheltered from the rain. After the eggs were laid, I theorized that the occasionally resident raccoon would kill the bird, eat the eggs spitting out the shells. I tried to explain this to the new owners, a newly arrived young Korean couple straight from the homeland. Their English was shaky. They simply couldn't grasp what kind of an animal a raccoon was so I, reaching for straws, allowed that raccoons were members of the bear family. They looked stricken upon hearing this news. Later, I remembered those wonderful, naïve antique paintings of Korean bears.

With the exception of raccoons, I've never found a live animal in a chimney. Although I keep looking for gold coins, jewelry or moonshine on smoke shelves—an obvious hiding place to me for things of value—I've never found any.

SUMMARY

Raccoons live inside chimneys on the smoke shelves of fireplaces. They raise their young there. Eviction strategies.

CHAPTER IX

EVOLUTION OF THE FIREPLACE

CONTENTS

Trying to reconstruct how a technology evolved during 500 years is not for the fainthearted.

Some years ago my wife and I visited a castle in Scotland, which had been built in the 15th century. Its center was a great hall, maybe 40' by 60', an enormous fireplace 12' wide and 6' high situated on the raised part at one end. When we stepped inside the fireplace, we could look up the flue and see lots of sky. This flue was exactly the same size as the fireplace opening, 12' by 6'!

The single greatest advance in fireplace design during the last 500 years has been the gradual *reduction of the ratio of fireplace opening to flue size*, which instead of being the same like the castle we visited, is now 10/1 or 12/1. This reduction has been made possible by several factors including better geometry, smaller fireplaces and *faster* starts, which heat the chimney more quickly and increase the draw. Individual but anonymous chimney and fireplace builders must be given credit here for experimentation and innovation. This is in line with what I spelled out in CHAPTER I: as soon as the chimney becomes warm, it draws so much harder that it can actually solve smoke problems.

We know that in England until perhaps 1740 grown men had swept chimneys, i.e., they climbed up inside the chimneys to do the work. Frequent sweeping/cleaning out of the unburned fuel residue—creosote from wood-burning or, if coal was the fuel, soot—from chimneys was an extremely important public safety measure to prevent big chimney fires. Creosote and soot are unburned but still flammable residues of incomplete combustion. Whole cities, typically then built almost exclusively of wood, were burned to the ground because a single chimney fire got out of control. Roofs were often made from thatch or wood shingles. Fire departments were the exception. Water was not usually available in large quantities and pumps, if they existed at all, were operated manually.

As fireplaces and flues became smaller and smaller, however, it became necessary to use very young (and small) children to perform the vital task. This must have been, to put it mildly, a very interesting period of transition. Child labor laws did not yet exist. The mortality rate for these tiny sweeps was very high yet the job they were performing made everyone much safer. The effort to ban the use of young children from the dangerous job of sweeping chimneys spurred one of the first citizen mass movements ever. It went on for more than 100 years until effective sweeping equipment was invented.

EVOLUTION STEPS

- *Starting about 1750, the fireplace to chimney flue ratio began to increase, from 1 to 1, to 12 to 1 today.*

- *The 19th century included the most dramatic changes. The idea that you could build fireplaces which did not smoke or smoked less drove lots of innovation, climaxing in the work of the Donley Brothers in Cleveland, Ohio, the first innovator to develop a detailed protocol for the design and construction to smoke-free fireplaces. The Donley's specialized in cast iron throat dampers, bringing them, in my view, to perfection. They codified fireplace dimensions, outside and interior, and apparently became the first to come up with recommended ratios of flues to fireplace openings. They invented the smoke chamber.*

- *A very important transition innovator was Count Rumford, who published his essay, "Of Chimney Fireplaces", in 1796. His signal contribution was proposing much greater splay to the sidewalls of fireplaces. This is the most important piece to making fireplaces smoke free. Rumford's ideas never took firm hold in the United States. England developed a variation of his fireplace which apparently worked well.*

- *There were important advances in the materials used in constructing fireplace systems. Cast iron firebacks became popular. Firebrick began to be manufactured mid-19th century, almost exclusively for industrial purposes.*

> By 1900, they were also used in fireplace construction, more or less replacing the fireback. Terra cotta flue liners were invented and were used in most fireplace chimney construction by 1900.
> - From roughly 1920 to 1950, building codes were written for fireplace construction. These codes increased the safety of fireplace systems.
> - During the 1950's and early '60's, fireplace glass doors became available. Top dampers first became available in the early 1970's.
> - Exhaust fans for fireplace chimneys became available in the 1990's.

OTHER CHANGES INFLUENCING FIREPLACES IN MID 18TH CENTURY

Wood was becoming scarce in England. Coal began to replace it. The society was changing because of the industrial revolution, increasing urban populations, and a growing middle class. Instead of a big fireplace in a great hall as we saw in the 15th century castle, the living room fireplace, in addition to heating, was becoming a focus of *domestic and family life*, actually very like its status today, hearth and home. In poorer households, the focus was the large kitchen fireplace, where cooking took place.

At the end of the 18th century it was further changed by Count Rumford's inspiration *to splay the angle of the sidewalls and to reduce the size of the throat.* Reducing the throat meant that less house air was also drawn up the chimney, one of the most serious flaws of fireplaces because it cools the whole house, as I've described, especially once the chimney gets warm.

When Count Rumford began to rebuild British fireplaces in the mid-1790's, many of them, apparently, were deep and square or rectangular. The fireplaces we see in the artistic representations of the time seem to have been around 36" wide or somewhat less. At first my thinking was that there were few rules for how to build a fireplace. But after thumbing through *The English Fireplace* by L.A. Shuffrey, I realized that even before Rumford, *modestly angling the sidewalls* was the practice in a significant percentage of fireplaces. But, mainly, attention and care was lavished on *the exterior* of the fireplace, how it looked. Rumford seems to be the first fireplace practitioner to exclusively address *interior fireplace geometry*. See Figure 60, from "Collected Works..." Volume II, Page 284 and 287.

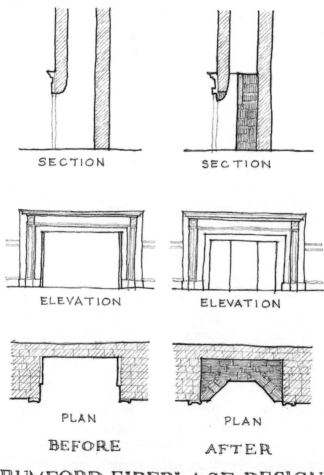

SECTION   SECTION

ELEVATION   ELEVATION

PLAN   PLAN

BEFORE   AFTER

RUMFORD FIREPLACE DESIGN

FIGURE 60

What Rumford recommended, however, was much *more severe splay*—135 degrees—than had ever before been proposed. He also made the fireplace shallow, actually a necessity if the splay is 135 degrees and the fireplace is 36" wide or less. Otherwise there is no back wall to speak of. The fuel, then in use, was bituminous coal, which is twice as dense as wood and requires a grate.

If we really wanted to know what Rumford accomplished, we would need to recreate the conditions he was confronted with: square fireboxes, little or no splay, huge throats, fireboxes much larger than the coal grates, soft coal, drafty houses, etc. Run such a fireplace and do lots of testing. And then modify it as he suggested and test that. These would be fascinating experiments.

In Rumford's classic paper, "Of Chimney Fireplaces," he registers that somewhat less splay than 135 degrees is acceptable. (Rumford justifies 135-degree splay because it will "cause the direct rays from the fire to be sent into the room by reflection in the greatest abundance.") If he's modifying a fireplace that smokes, he says that he splays the sidewalls *less* than 135, why he never explains. It is possible that 135 degrees was sometimes pushing a good thing a little too far and that, if there were other factors, like slightly lower than normal air pressure in the fireplace room or random modest gusts of air from doors opening and closing, the fireplace would smoke a little less. There may just be a sweet spot for splay, possibly 125 degrees, which garners most of splay's benefits and yet is more robust on other scores than 135 degrees.

In the United States, Rumford's modifications of the fireplace were further modified, starting perhaps with Thomas Jefferson who, after reading Rumford's original essay and consulting with his architect, reduced Rumford's splay to around 120 degrees to accommodate the burning of wood in the comparatively deep Monticello fireplaces 36" wide. I'm assuming that regular firewood was, at that time, cut in 2' or slightly shorter lengths, just as it is today. (This would be in accord with the measurement of a cord, which is 4' by 4' by 8', each piece of wood supposedly being a full 2'. Measuring wood by the cord goes back to 17th century Britain.)

Rumford's modifications came in mathematical terms: the width of the fireplace was to be three times its depth and the width and height of the opening were to be the same, or square. Furthermore, the width of the back wall was to be the same as the depth. This resulted, as you saw above, in a much shallower fireplace, with deeply splayed sidewalls. Proposing *proportional* fireplace dimensions was a new idea. Modifying the splay to 120 degrees, as Jefferson and other Americans did, changed these proportional dimensions, widening the back wall and permitting increased fireplace depth.

There is not agreement if Rumford proposed a plumb back wall or a pitched or slanted wall. It is true that Rumford *mentions* slanting the back wall to solve a particular smoke problem but he never shows it graphically. All the lithographs he includes in "Of Chimney Fireplaces" show plumb back walls. Historians writing about fireplaces recommend a forward-leaning back wall leading into the damper opening and credit Rumford for it.

The other Rumford proposal, also seen in his lithographs, is the *rounded chimneybreast*. Some Rumford enthusiasts believe this improves the performance of the fireplace, why they don't say. But Rumford gives another reason: "If the under side of the mantle be left broad and flat, it is easy to perceive that the cloud of dust or light ashes that rises from a coal fire nearly burned out when it is violently stirred with a poker, striking perpendicularly against this flat part of it, must unavoidably be beat back into the room; but when the breast of the chimney is properly rounded off, the ascending cloud of dust and smoke more easily finds its way into the throat of the chimney...." Ibid, Page 298-299.

Rumford's assertion that *any hindrance* on the back wall would create smoking is, in my experience, simply not true if there is sufficient splay to the sidewalls. And even Rumford contradicts himself on this issue. In a fascinating footnote, he describes angling the *lower back wall* of a fireplace to accommodate an oversize grate and that it greatly increased heat output. See Figure 61.

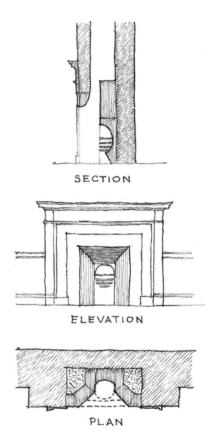

SECTION

ELEVATION

PLAN

RUMFORD FIREPLACE DESIGN WITH LARGE COAL GRATE

FIGURE 61

Although he says this phenomenon should be investigated further, he never writes about it again, a great pity. He also never corrects himself on the issue of an angled back wall or acknowledges that he has contradicted himself.

Fireplaces Rumfordized—yes, the process was actually called that—in the early 19th century that I have seen in historic houses in the United States all have the increased splay but not to 135 degrees but to 120 to 125. Usually the back wall is slightly angled starting 1/3 or more of the way up. One example of this is a beautiful heavily-used fireplace I rebuilt on the Eastern Shore of Maryland's Chesapeake Bay, which has a *severely* angled back wall starting above an 18" high cast iron fire-back. The sidewalls are 120 degrees and smoke exits the firebox all the way to the front. I find it instructive that this quintessential Rumford, as far as I could determine, never had a rounded chimneybreast and worked flawlessly for a couple of hundred years and will continue to do so for the next. There was no trace of smoke stains on the surround or mantel.

One of the most interesting parts of this job was that there was an identical fireplace about 8 feet away on the same wall, which had not been Rumfordized. There were no signs that it had ever been used.

What I've asked myself many times is whether Rumford grasped that 135 degree splay actually increased the draw of the chimney and consequently prevented smoking. Rumford certainly never says as much. He knew it increased the amount of heat radiated by the fireplace. It made the fireplace more efficient, he asserts. But I wonder why he thought his fireplaces did not smoke. As I noted earlier, he only says *one time—once—*that increasing the splay solved smoke problems and, in my view, he only says it indirectly, almost obliquely, no pun intended. Because this is such an important idea, I'm quoting the excerpt in full, starting with his comments on the fireplaces of his day: "First, in a fireplace so constructed, the sides of the fireplace—or covings, as they are called—are parallel to each other, and consequently ill contrived to throw out into the room the heat they receive from the fire in the form of rays; and secondly, the large open corners, which are formed by making the back as wide as the opening of the fireplace in front, *occasion eddies of wind which frequently disturb the fire, and embarrass the smoke in its ascent in such a manner as* *often to bring it into the room. Both these defects may be entirely remedied by diminishing the width of the back of the fireplace."* (My italics.) (Pages 248-249.) Diminishing the width of the back wall, of course, *increases the splay*. I wish Rumford hadn't used a circumlocution to say this.

It may be that splay is most important *before* the chimney has heated up much and begins drawing hard and the slant of the back wall most important for radiating heat once the chimney is hot. In my opinion, both good splay and angling of the back wall significantly increase radiant heat output. (More about good splay in a moment.)

My sense of Rumford's achievement was that he put his finger on two of the most important variables in fireplace construction: the angle of the sidewalls and the size of the throat, the latter a subject he was addressing right before the above quotation.

AMERICAN FIREPLACES

We have to remember that Americans had always been very advanced in their fireplace designs. In fact, one Rumford critic of their time complained that Rumford had presented fireplace designs as his own which were already the practice in America. I believe the aspect of the Rumford fireplace this critic was referring to is the splay or angle of the sidewalls. Evidence supporting this opinion can be found in the photographs of William Morgan's *A Simpler Way of Life: Old Farmhouses of New York and New England,* which feature many fireplaces with very generous splay, some apparently even greater than 125 degrees. Most of them were built pre-Rumford, i.e., before 1800, according to dates given in the text. I can't tell from the photographs if the back walls are also angled forward but I strongly suspect they are. I would like to know what other parts of the country have to offer for pre-Rumford fireplaces. Might the US Park Service be interested in conducting a countrywide survey?

It makes sense to me that American fireplace builders always built with lots of splay and, most likely, angled forward back walls because our climate, at least in the northern part of the country, required lots of heating during the winter months— much more than England's—and most of our heaters were fireplaces. I've read that Rumford, an extraordinarily precocious child, loved nothing more than watching workmen at work. I believe he saw a fireplace (or fireplaces) being built when he was a boy—he grew up in New England—and noticed the splay and then, probably, also asked the workmen about it. There is a good chance, I believe, that the Rumford critic mentioned above was right on.

Where I have started is fixing smoking fireplaces with splay occasionally less than 100 degrees and frequently less than 110. Increasing these splays 10, 15, 20, even 25 degrees has, as I've explained earlier, *always* decreased smoking problems and usually solved them completely, even major ones.

The other interesting part of Rumford's designs is *the restriction through the damper or opening to the chimney.* For instance, if the fireplace opening is 36" by 36", the damper opening might end up 4" by 20". A regular fireplace, without the rounded chimneybreast, where the damper sits against the *front wall*, would have a damper opening of 4" by 30", which makes the damper opening 50% greater, or, from the opposite perspective, the Rumford damper opening 50% smaller.

Yet my experiments using a heat probe and regular throat damper showed no temperature increase with my heat probe when the damper opening was only halved. When I more than halved the opening, I saw temperature increases. But then the fireplace began to smoke. Using a top damper allows much greater restriction, as I described in Chapter V.

The issue is one of efficiency: the more restricted the damper opening, at least theoretically, the more efficient the fireplace because less house air is also drawn up the chimney.

Rumford was well aware how inefficient the fireplaces of his day were. I am struck by his environmental consciousness, which connects combustion inefficiency and pollution. Most people consider this a very modern idea. Rumford claims that the waste of fuel in his time is enormous, reaching as high as 7/8th. A particularly eloquent passage of his reads as follows: "The enormous waste of fuel in London may be estimated by the vast dark cloud which continually hangs over this great metropolis, and frequently overshadows the whole country, far and wide; for this dense cloud is certainly composed almost entirely of *unconsumed coal*, (Rumford's emphasis, not mine) which, having stolen wings from the innumerable fires of this great city, has escaped by the chimneys, and continues to sail about in the air, till, having lost the heat which gave it volatility, it falls in a dry shower of extremely fine black dust to the ground, obscuring the atmosphere in its descent, and, frequently changing the brightest day into more than Egyptian darkness." (Ibid, 181-182.) Rumford was convinced that his fireplaces were more efficient and less polluting. I suspect he was right. I showed in Chapter V that greater efficiency is also possible.

HOW RUMFORD INFLUENCED 19TH CENTURY FIREPLACES

What happened with Rumford's proposals, according Frederick Edwards, Junior, a fireplace and heating expert in 19th century England, is the adoption of the extreme splay, which appears from the following drawings to be almost 150 degrees, at *the mouth* of the fireplace. Deeper into the firebox, the splay seems to have been reduced to around 135 degrees. A damper was installed—then called a regulator—which could be easily and precisely manipulated from outside the fireplace. The rounded chimneybreast was not attempted. Edwards opens his pamphlet, *A Treatise on Smoky Chimneys, Their Cure and Prevention*, as follows:

"About seventy years ago smoky chimneys in England were so common an evil, that not only were there no houses without them, but the chimney that would *draw* well in all states of the atmosphere, without the temporary assistance of an open window, was exceedingly rare. Count Rumford appeared, and in essays which have gained esteem for the author of them, wherever they have been perused, established rules for the construction of our fireplaces, which have procured for us the very large amount of fire-side comfort we now possess. In the course of fifty years, a smoky or doubtful chimney became the exception instead of the rule..."

According to Edward's drawings, shown below, smoke exited at the *back* of the fireplace, not the front, and not even at the highest point of the firebox. To me, the firebox had become a severe cone or funnel lying on its side, with a coal grate slightly raised. How this fireplace differed from Rumford's is that the strong splay was not only on the sides but *also on the top.* I have never seen one of these fireplaces.

I can imagine these fireplaces working *once a chimney were warm.* But I would think it might be challenging to get them started. These fireplaces were constructed of firebrick not metal or cast iron, per Rumford's instructions. I found it intriguing that Edwards says the damper can be closed about 2/3rds "as soon as the coal is well ignited." Assuming this to be true, it follows that Edward's lead cause of smoking, the 1st on his list of 15, is "from a fireplace being too open." I didn't understand right away that, to Frederick, "too open" meant without splay or without enough splay, i.e., too large *on the inside* of the firebox. See Figure 62.

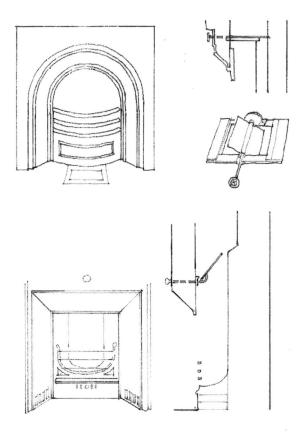

RUMFORD STYLE COAL FIREPLACES
IN MID~19th CENTURY BRITAIN
FIGURE 62

Edwards does not to give specific dimensions, although he must have known them. I suppose the main point of a drawing like this is to show the proportions of the different parts.

Notice that the splay of the lower fireplace shown in Figure 62 is mainly at the front of the firebox. (It's hard to determine how much angle there is deeper inside.) According to the drawing the outer angle is more than 130 degrees. With the upper fireplace, the outer angle is closer to150! The drawing below shows a fireplace with *outside splay* at almost 145 degrees. The inside seems to have extremely modest splay if any. See Figure 63.

SMALL, DEEP FIREPLACE WITH LARGE OUTSIDE SPLAY

FIGURE 63

The *outside splay* appears to be another solution to the challenge of narrow fireboxes, where I proposed, in Chapter II, the mermaid fireplace.

When I first began to explore splay, I'd assumed it would only be *inside splay*, i.e., splay inside the deepest part of the firebox. It never occurred to me that *outside splay* might also be an option. I have no idea if they have equal power. But the drawings and the picture of an existing, apparently functional fireplace suggest they are comparable.

Edwards, who owned a company that specialized in the manufacture and sale of coal grates, wrote several excellent pamphlets, including the one quoted above, *A Treatise on Smoky Chimneys....*, *On Domestic Use of Fuel and on Ventilation*, and *The Extravagant Use of Fuel in Cooking Operations.* These pamphlets went through several editions. They were published in England in the mid-1860s.

My conclusion from reading Edward's writings is that Rumford made a huge impact on the design of British fireplaces, making them more efficient and more reliable. I don't believe, however, that these Rumford-influenced innovations ever took hold in the United States in part because our fuel was different. Until at least 1885, firewood was plentiful and available here. In Britain, the main fuel had been coal since around 1750. I believe we took a different route and tried to design cast-iron and metal inserts for our fireplaces. One of the few I've ever seen is the famous Latrobe, which may have worked more or less, but which I found overly complicated.

My chief piece of evidence for Americans not grasping the essence of Rumford is the book, *The Open Fireplace In All Ages* by J. Pickering Putnam, which was published in 1880. Putnam's book covers three areas. The first is his documentation of the horrible inefficiencies of American fireplaces; he takes extensive measurements of the temperatures of flue gasses coming out the tops of chimneys, showing how wasteful our heating was. (Putnam never mentions the 19th century evolution of the English fireplace. Apparently, he was unfamiliar with Edward's pamphlets and the fireplace designs I have just shown.) The second is an inventory of fireplace decorative treatments, probably intended to function as the sales tool for his book. And, third, he describes and analyzes different mechanical solutions to increasing fireplace efficiencies. This is an important record showing the enormous difficulty of making open fireplaces *at all efficient*. Putnam was obviously well aware of the contradiction. On the one hand, humans strongly prefer the open fire. That's where our hearts lie. On the other hand, the challenges are many. As I showed in Chapter V, the use of the top damper and the single brick chimneybreast are two of the keys to real improvement.

ADVENT OF CENTRAL HEATING

Central heating was starting up in Europe in the late 18th century, pretty much at the same time as Rumford was doing his pioneering fireplace work. It is interesting to me that Rumford must have really *loved* open fireplaces. (Or he realized that everyone else loved open fireplaces...) Otherwise, he would probably have put his extraordinary energy and brainpower into central heating systems, or masonry stoves, both of which he must have known about. (He did lots of work on cook stoves, designing them for much higher efficiencies and greater convenience.)

Central heating came to the United States later than Europe. The White House, for example, did not have it until 1891. Early central heating in the United States was fueled by wood or coal furnaces, *the hot air distributed by convection*. (I used one of these by-then ancient coal-burning systems in the late 1960s. The only way heat got into the house was through a 36" by 36" hot air grate in the front hallway at the bottom of the stairs to the 2nd floor. The furnace was directly below, in the cellar.) I believe this method, a necessity before the widespread availability of electricity to power fans, was one of the reasons that fireplace dampers became so important. To properly heat a whole house by convection, it simply had to be more or less closed, i.e., much more airtight than had been the practice before.

DONLEY BROTHERS

Enter the Donley Brothers, who, among many others, had begun casting fireplace dampers and other fireplace equipment at their foundries in Cleveland, Ohio, in the 1890's. This era, the end of the century was experiencing a revival of the open fireplace as an *architectural feature,* i.e., something pleasing to the eye. But it also had to function as a fireplace that didn't smoke. *I don't think anyone still imagined it would ever be used as a serious heater.*

In other words, the revival was mainly cultural, visual, decorative. You needed a fireplace to *anchor how the most important rooms in your house looked,* especially the living room and dining room, to give these important rooms that traditional focus. The proliferation of damper manufacturers and designs at this time can be explained by this new requirement—the ability to close off the fireplace chimney, i.e., to prevent the chimney from drawing air out of the house when the fireplace was not in use and yet preserve the option of occasional use. An open fireplace chimney can be very wasteful of house air and heat, as I mentioned above, and can end up neutralizing the benefits of central heating. (All of us moderns should take note of this fact, which is still true today.) For a new technology to be credible, it has to work well. I also think our standards of comfort escalated. We wanted our dwellings to be warmer, lots warmer. But we weren't willing to give up the open fireplace.

These Donley's were, I believe, the most sophisticated and most important fireplace pioneers of their time. Their business model, as we might say today, was to make their fireplaces completely reliable for *intermittent* use. I understand that they actually tested their damper designs and the best firebox designs. They were also familiar with Rumford's proposals.

But it's clear that the Donley's read Rumford critically, accepting some of his proposals and rejecting others, testing as they went. Unfortunately, the man who bought their company in the 1970's burned all the Donley research papers, a great loss to fireplace history and evolution.

There are, however, some hints to their thinking because the Donley's published a sales manual, *Book of Successful fireplaces, How To Build Them*, starting before 1910 and continued periodically every few years for more than 60 years. In the manual they give their *recommended dimensions and geometry* for fireplaces of different sizes using the Donley dampers, the numbers presumably derived from their own experiments. To my knowledge, there had been nothing like this since Rumford's *proportionality dimensions*.

In his book, *The American Fireplace*, Henry J. Kauffman implicitly endorses the Donley's when he writes, "For many years fireplaces were built on hearsay methods, which has led to the construction of devices stingy with heat and productive of smoke. Hopefully, such a result will be avoided,..." Page 175. He then proceeds to reprint verbatim some 10 pages of the most important directions found in the Donley's *Book of Successful Fireplaces*, without giving any attribution.

When Kauffman says that fireplaces "were built on hearsay methods," this is my strong impression as well. In fact, I would venture that too many fireplaces are *today still* "built on hearsay methods." As I've described at many points in this book, both architects and fireplace builders simply don't appreciate the importance of key aspects of firebox design. Usually, this is not willfulness or laziness. It is based on ignorance, pure and simple, on hearsay.

By 1920, I believe every architect in America had at least two copies of the Donley manual, which they would consult whenever they were designing a fireplace for a customer. Architectural Graphic Standards, the architect's Bible today, didn't begin to publish until the late 1930's and, for some 25 years thereafter, included a section specifically on Donley fireplaces using Donley's numbers and illustrations.

In addition, the Donley's book gave readers lots and lots of general fireplace information and ideas about different styles of fireplaces. (I'm sure the architects always loaned the booklet to their customers.) To give you a sense of this as a sales tool, I'm listing a Table of Contents from the 1929 Edition of their book. See Figure 64.

Table of Contents

Subject	*Page*
Living Room Fireplaces	4
Fireplace History	5
Bedroom Fireplaces	20
Library and Den Fireplaces	22
Porch and Basement Fireplaces	23
Summer Cottage and Cabin Fireplaces	24
Public Building Fireplaces	26
Apartment House Fireplaces	28
Ready-Made Fireplaces	29
Fireplace Construction Plans	30
Fireplace Equipment	43
How Not to Build a Fireplace	50
A Portfolio of Fireplace Designs	52
Fireplace Building for Amateurs	66
Where to Get Donley Fireplace Equipment	18, 37

FIGURE 64

These books included scores of black and white photographs of different-looking finished fireplaces and literally hundreds of drawings of various brick front treatments.

One of the most endearing parts of the publication was its low-key quality. In the 1929 edition, for example, there appears the following sentences: "This equipment can easily be had from your local Building Supply Dealer. At this point we would like to insert a word of warning. Do not take it for granted that other equipment will work well with these plans, nor that this equipment will work well with other plans, for such may not be the case. The two combined, however, will produce a successful fireplace." The above does not appear until Page 18. (That year, the book was under 70 pages; eventually it grew to over 100 pages, as the Donley's added new fireplace articles and equipment.)

Its title, *"Book of Successful Fireplaces, How to Build Them,"* is striking the perfect pose: there's the implication that there are lots and lots of *unsuccessful* fireplaces out there. Under its breath, the book was saying, "Let us show you how to get your fireplace right!"

The most important part, however, which was the basis for their instructions on the sizing and geometry of fireplaces, is well-hidden—on a par with a trade secret—and has understandably gone unnoticed for more than 100 years. It is *the angle they selected for the sidewalls, the degree of splay.* The Donley's, I'm sure after much testing of different splay geometries, including Rumford's, picked what they must have considered the *most practical* angle of splay for the sidewalls of a fireplace. I have done the math and it's 110 degrees. (Unlike Rumford, they didn't put a degree number on it.) My contention is that, had they picked a greater angle, say 115, 120, 125, 130, etc., their recommended fireplace dimensions would have been very different because they would have registered the effect of the *increased air pressure at the back wall,* which makes a fireplace chimney draw significantly harder. It's likely that the Donley's understood that greater draw could be a liability. More on this in a moment.

About the time the Donley's started casting dampers, flue liners were invented. The Donley's were the first fireplace group to specify what size fireplace opening worked best with what size flue liner. As far as I can determine, it was from the Donley's that we get the 10 to 1 ratio for medium tall chimneys and 12 to 1 for tall chimneys. We also have the Donley's to thank for the concept of the smoke chamber.

DONLEY CARTOONS

Included in their informative manual (Sixth Edition)—actually the first-ever version of a coffee table fireplace book I've ever seen—but much more technical because it included their instructions for fireplace dimensions and construction, there were a couple of pages of cartoons for what *not* to do when designing or building a fireplace. See Figure 65 for cartoons shown in their damper installation instructions.

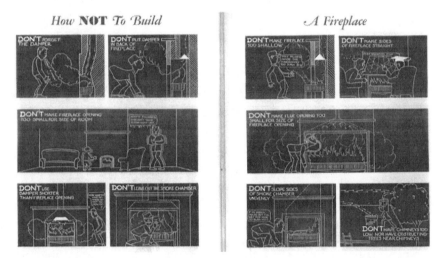

FIGURE 65

I find these cartoons remarkably comprehensive about the design and construction *mistakes that lead to smoking*—literally 9 out of 10 are about smoking. This fits into my theory that the Donley booklets zero in on the distinct possibility of ending up with an *unsuccessful* fireplace, i.e., one that smoked. The only important recommendation they did not include is the height of the damper above the fireplace opening. (They mention this elsewhere.) The only cartoon I don't agree with is the one showing nearby trees causing smoking. In my experience trees, deciduous or evergreen, don't create any problems because a chimney is driven by heat and the difference in air pressure. Even on a windy day, trees never seem to cause smoking, why I'm not quite sure. Maybe it's only solid objects which actually block the wind completely that cause downdrafts. Tree foliage is not a solid object.

A curious omission from the cartoons listed *in their manuals* is the one titled, "Don't Make Sides of Fireplace Straight." It is only listed in the damper *installation* instructions attached to each damper sold. I don't know why they neglected to include it in their booklet. It is possible that this most important piece of information, which could be of great value to their competition, if they really understood it, was intentionally omitted.

These cartoons, I believe, were in large part directed at the consumer, who was having a fireplace designed and built. They presented vital information in a way that virtually anyone could understand and no serious person/consumer could ignore. They strongly conveyed the idea that there is a right way and a wrong way to build a fireplace. (Rumford's rules had been more or less forgotten.) Fireplace builders were suddenly being asked by architects and homeowners to build fireplaces in a certain way, a new way. By explaining fireplaces so well, Donley was showing consumers great respect. To me, it feels like democracy/capitalism at their best. (Compare Donley's splay to other damper manufacturers, using Mac's old Graphic Standards.)

Used Donley books can still sometimes be bought on Amazon for a song.

DONLEY MECHANISMS
The brothers also invented damper controls called Donley mechanisms. Once you've mastered the mechanism's action, they prove to be the best damper controls ever made. The outstanding feature is that you can achieve the lowest setting almost effortlessly at the end of a fire. Using a fireplace poker with a hook on it, you close it all the way and then pull down slightly until it clicks. That's a little less than ½" open, just what we want. See Figure 66.

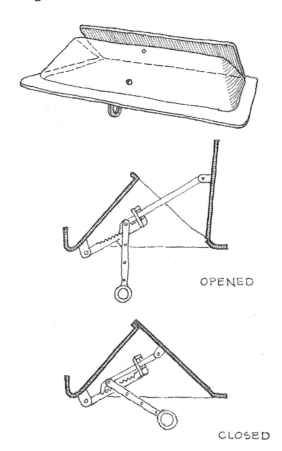

OPENED

CLOSED

DONLEY MECHANISM
DAMPER CONTROL

FIGURE 66

Donley "mechanisms" work in any position. Their only weakness is that their motion is counterintuitive: You push the handle upwards slightly and away from you to close the damper and you pull it slightly down and towards you to open it. There is definitely a learning curve to master it.

The Donley Company, having had several owners since the brothers died, was until recently the Allied Dealers Supply Company. It declared bankruptcy in 2011. In my opinion, this is the second tragedy for the Donley's legacy and for all fireplace builders and for fireplace technology in general. (The first, as I mentioned, is that their research papers were destroyed.)

When I first began building fireboxes in the early 1980's, most brickyards carried the Donley-Allied along with other dampers. But they hated carrying more than one brand. When they suddenly cut back on the Donley-Allied, perhaps because Allied didn't continue publication of Donley's *Book of Successful Fireplaces,* I'd argue with them that it was the better damper and here's why. They'd just look at me as if I were some poor nitwit. They seemed to enjoy thwarting me. To them, all fireplace dampers were basically the same. How could these small differences make such a big difference? Starting around then, I had to order Allied dampers specially—several hundred over the next 30 years.

I fault Allied for poor management and poor public relations. There wasn't any price difference between the dampers. I don't think Allied ever grasped what a good product the Donley Brothers had created.

We can say in hindsight that the real problem was the general murkiness around the innards of fireplaces. Had the Donley's research papers survived, these could have been used to build a case for the Donley designs.

RUMFORD FIREPLACES TODAY

The most influential Rumford expert today, Jim Buckley, believes that Rumford fireplaces should have *plumb* back walls and fat, rounded chimneybreasts but not the 135-degree splay to the sidewalls, which his fireplace dimension chart shows clocking in at around 125 degrees. Buckley's Rumford is very similar to Rumford's except there is no smoke shelf. In cooperation with the Superior Clay Corporation, Mr. Buckley has designed and tested a Rumford Fireplace Kit, which includes components for *his fat* chimneybreast, a lower damper of his own design—Rumford had no damper although he wrote about its potential utility—a terra cotta smoke chamber assembly, and complete construction instructions. Buckley has made a very important contribution to modern fireplace design by reviving our interest in Rumford's proposals and making Rumford components available.

I strongly agree with Buckley on setting the splay of the side walls to 125 degree although, as I mentioned in Chapter V, increasing the splay much beyond 110 or 115 degrees and not also installing a good top damper, may strengthen the chimney so much that's its natural inefficiency is increased. As I've mentioned in Chapter V, I have found that angled and even stepped back walls make fireplaces more efficient. My 3rd disagreement with Buckley is regarding the lack of a smoke shelf. In my experience, it's safer to have the opening from the firebox to the smoke chamber towards the front so that a big chimney fire can't fall into the firebox, or at least not much of it.

Not withstanding my reservations about these issues, Buckley's Rumford fireplaces work very reliably, in large part, it is my belief, because of their good splay. But, as I mentioned in Chapter V, I would be very interested to see how much the use of a top damper affected their heat output. I suspect that it could be dramatic, dramatically improved.

Another style of Rumford built today, without using Buckley's kit, does not have the fat rounded chimneybreast but does have an angled or sloped back wall. The smoke exit—today, a throat damper—is all the way forward and specially fashioned for each fireplace. This style of Rumford is very like the early19th century Rumford fireplace I rebuilt on Maryland's Eastern Shore.

As I've described in Chapter V, I believe the next obvious step in fireplace evolution
Is tapping the heat of the flue gasses by reducing the thickness of the chimneybreast to a single brick. In combination with the top damper open fireplaces could then be made much more efficient.

Testing the efficiency of these different-style, top-dampered fireplaces with heat probe systems and possibly other equipment is a necessity.

Summary

The main way fireplaces have evolved is by becoming smaller with much smaller flues. Before around 1700 grown men could still sweep chimneys: the flues were big enough. By 1800, chimneys were swept by young children. It was dangerous, unhealthy work and spawned one of the first citizen mass movements ever. Coal had supplanted wood by 1750. Count Rumford arrived on the scene in the 1790's. The chief part of his proposal was to greatly increase the splay of the sidewalls of the fireplace. Rumford was the first to propose mathematical proportions to fireplaces. Rebuilding along the lines he had proposed was called Rumfordization, both in England and the US. Jefferson was a proponent of modified Rumford fireplaces. Fast forward to the end of the 19th century when a company, the Donley Brothers, began casting fireplace dampers in Cleveland. The Donley's dominated American fireplace construction for 70 years by proposing exact specifications for successful fireplaces. Donley fireplace cartoons telling how not to build a fireplace. The most efficient fireplaces of the future will have a one-brick chimneybreast for tapping flue gas heat.

CHAPTER X

REVIEW OF CENTRAL POINTS

- Chimneys draw much harder when hot.
- Fireplace geometry is important, especially the splay of the sidewalls.
- There are two main kinds of smoking, structural and systemic.
- Short fireplace chimneys don't start well.
- Other fireplace deficiencies explained, poor screens, lack of air, etc.
- Fireplace evolution has meant smaller and smaller flues and greater ratios.
- Hot fireplace chimneys can be severely restricted with top dampers, making fireplaces better heaters.
- If building a fireplace system from scratch or engaged in extensive renovation, *build the chimney breast one layer of brick only, not two or three as with conventional chimney construction.* This should greatly increase the heat output of the fireplace and make top damper restriction even more effective.
- Fireplaces are remarkably safe if constructed according to code, which most are.
- Trees to be used for firewood should be cut down when the sap is in the roots.
- Raccoons love fireplaces as much as we do but for different reasons.

At the beginning of the book, I showed the master plan for a typical fireplace/chimney system. I'm showing it again alongside a master plan for an *improved* fireplace/chimney system. (Both are exterior chimney systems.) These improved systems will start better, be less likely to smoke, radiate more heat, be safer and be less likely to need sweeping. They will, however, require homeowners to understand and operate them in a certain way. See Figure 67.

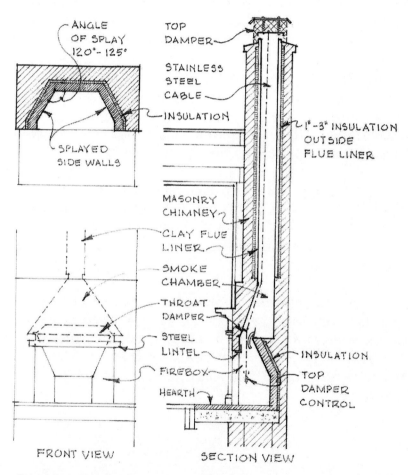

IMPROVED MASONRY FIREPLACE CHIMNEY SYSTEM

FIGURE 67

To repeat the description I gave at the beginning of the book about fireplaces:

A fireplace/chimney system has two distinct parts: the firebox where burning takes place and a duct or channel for removing smoke and gasses, the chimney flue. The two are not the same size. The firebox opening is usually 10 (or 12) times as large as the interior cross-section of the chimney flue. This is known as the fireplace to chimney ratio. The genius of a fireplace is that it has 3 points of transition where smoke and gasses are funneled into smaller spaces. They are in the firebox, (1) where the angled sidewalls form a funnel leading to the back wall and into the throat; (2) where the throat forms a funnel leading into the damper opening; and (3) where the smoke chamber funnels into the flue liner. Without this funneling, the chimney would have to be as large as the fireplace opening, the design of some early fireplace/chimney systems. See opening of Chapter V.

I have added a 4th point of transition, of funneling, if you will, with the top damper. So instead of fireplace to chimney ratio being 10 to 1 (or, 12 to 1 for tall chimneys), it has theoretically become, with hot chimneys, at least 30 to 1 with the help of top damper restriction.

By making the smoke chamber only one brick thickness away from the room with the fireplace, we have in effect placed an enormous masonry radiator in our living room, which taps the flue gasses in the chimney and radiates heat many hours after the fire has gone out. This opens a new chapter for the masonry fireplace.

CHAPTER XI

SUPPLIERS

A great loss is that Allied Dealers went bankrupt and Donley-style dampers are no longer available. In addition to being less deep than the other available dampers, 9" instead of 12", Allied (and Donley before them) made a damper for fireplaces 33" wide, something no other company does or did. We can only hope that Allied will make it back in some form or other.

The best top damper brand, RMR, doesn't sell to the general public To obtain RMR top dampers, you will have to work with a chimney sweep or contractor. As I said before, I believe the RMR top damper is probably the best, mainly because of its ball-control mechanism. But lots of the other dampers are good products. The one I've used the most—this was before RMR came on the scene—is the Chimalator, the first company to make a top damper. They have completely redesigned their damper twice over the last 20 years! Its controls are the most user-friendly but, as I've mentioned, they are nowhere near as precise and continuous as RMR's. I hope Chimalator will redesign their controls.

For smoke plates, the Chimalator Company (a division of Bernard Dalsin Manufacturing) has the largest selection, from 3", 4.5", 6", and 8", adjustable from 24" wide to 52". This design can be adjusted to width with its long threaded rod. All the plates are painted flat black. The HY-C Company has three sizes, 4", 6" and 8", adjustable from 28.5" to 48". All three sizes are available in black. The 4" plate is also available in brass. This design of smoke plate pressure-fits with a spring. Remember to use the enclosed insulation to protect the spring from the heat! HY-C sells to the general public. Their phone number is 800-325-7076 and their web site, www.hyccompany.com.

Smoke plates are also widely available from hardware and fireplace stores and on the web.

True grates are also available from HY-C. There are other fine tall, true grates, which most fireplace stores stock. Vestal makes a fine grate. Remember: 4" tall and small openings to hold the live coals. If you're planning on running your fireplace for more than 3 hours, i.e., more like a heater, it's probably advisable to get what they call dog log rests, firedogs, or dog irons, which I show in Chapter V. A long fire will overwhelm (and probably melt) any standard grate by producing large quantities of hot coals.

Glass doors are available from virtually every fireplace store. It's their best selling product. The criteria I use to evaluate them are the strength of the outside frame and looks. Being a purist, I favor a plain-looking glass door with a narrow outside frame because it detracts less from the primordial flavor of a fireplace. It's important to discuss the situation with a knowledgeable fireplace equipment salesman before making a purchase. The same would apply, for different reasons, to exhaust fans, which are often installed for similar reasons.

When attaching glass doors in the most permanent way, I like to use masonry anchors, light dog chain, and aluminum turnbuckles to attach the glass door frame to the brick sidewalls. The threaded clasps included with the doors typically become loose after one or two seasons because of the heating and cooling cycles and the fiddling involved with the opening and closing of the doors. See Figure 68.

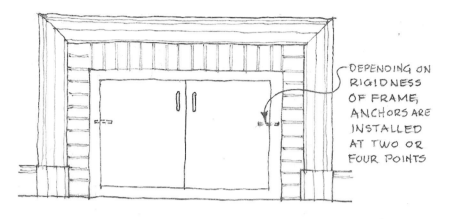

DEPENDING ON
RIGIDNESS
OF FRAME,
ANCHORS ARE
INSTALLED
AT TWO OR
FOUR POINTS

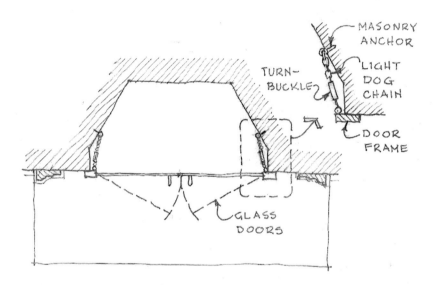

MASONRY
ANCHOR

TURN-
BUCKLE

LIGHT
DOG
CHAIN

DOOR
FRAME

GLASS
DOORS

ALTERNATIVE GLASS DOOR INSTALLATION

FIGURE 68

If you want to buy a cord or more of firewood, I would go to the yellow pages or web and buy mid or late summer. Someone who is in this business will know what you're talking about when you specify that you want wood that was cut when the sap was in the roots. If they seem at all confused, call someone else.

BIBLIOGRAPHY

Cullingford, Benita. *British Chimney Sweeps*. Great Britain: The Book Guild LTD, 2000.

Donley Brothers. *Book of Successful Fireplaces, How to Build Them*. Cleveland, OH: The Donley Brothers Company, 1947.

Edwards, Frederick. *Treatise on Smoky Chimneys: Their Cure and Prevention; the Utilization of Waste Heat from Open Fireplaces*. Great Britain, 1863-1870.

Gauger, Nicholas. *The Mechanism of Fire Made in Chimneys*. London, 1716.

Gay, Larry. *Heating With Wood*. Charlotte, VT: Garden Way Publishing, 1974.

Kauffman, Henry J.. *The American Fireplace*. New York: Galahad, 1972.

Kern, Ken & Magers, Steve. *Fireplaces*. Oakhurst, CA: Owner Builder Publications, 1978.

Kern, Ken. *The Masonry Stove*. New York: Charles Scribner's Sons, 1983.

Lyle, David. *The Book of Masonry Stoves*. White River Junction, VT: Chelsea Green Publishing, 1984.

Matesz, Ken. *Masonry Heaters*. White River Junction, VT: Chelsea Green Publishing, 2010.

Morgan, William. *A Simpler Way of Life: Old Farmhouses of New York and New England*. Bovina, NY: Norfleet Press, 2013.

Morstead, H.. *Fireplace Technology in an Energy Conscious World*. Calgary, Alberta, Canada: Centre for Research and Development in Masonry, 1981.

Orton, Vrest. *The Forgotten Art of Building a Good Fireplace.* Dublin, NH: Yankee Inc., 1974.

Putnam, J. Pickering. *The Open Fireplaces in All Ages.* Boston, MA: James R. Osgood & Company, 1880.

Rosin, P.O.. "The Aerodynamics of Domestic Open Fireplaces," *Journal of the Institute of Fuel*; Vol. 12; 1939, pp 198-224.

Rumford, Count. *Collected Works of Count Rumford, Volume 2: Practical Applications of Heat.* Cambridge, MA: Belknap Press, 1969.

Shelton, Jay. *Solid Fuels Encyclopedia.* Pownal, VT: Storey Communications, 1983

Shelton, Jay. *The Woodburners Encyclopedia.* Waitsfield, VT: Vermont Crossroads Press, 1976.

Shuffrey, L. A.. *The English Fireplace.* Great Britain: B.T. Batsford, 1912.

Warren, David J.. *Energy Efficient Masonry Fireplace: Design and Performance Evaluation.* Calgary, Alberta, Canada: Centre for Research and Development in Masonry, 1983.

INDEX

S

sap, 156, 161, 203

screening, 91

smoke chamber, 35, 66, 70, 72, 88, 124, 126, 128–29, 131, 173, 192, 196, 200

opening, 88

smoke crossover, 70, 73, 124

smoke plate, 10, 12, 17, 19, 22, 38, 66, 81–82, 95–98, 100, 107, 201–2

smoke shelf, 95, 145–46, 163–64, 166–67, 170, 196

smoking, 79–80, 84, 108, 198

smoking problem, xi-xii, 3, 8-9, 12-14, 17, 19, 22, 28, 32, 34-35, 45, 66, 73, 76, 79-80, 82, 83, 84, 85, 105, 108, 109, 143-144, 172, 198

sniff test, 80, 119–20

soot, 172

sparks, 161

splay, 19, 22, 24, 32–33, 36, 183, 197

power of, 19, 23, 32

structural smoking problem, 22, 53

systemic smoking, 18, 37-41, 43, 48, 53-54, 62, 63, 65, 66, 67, 72, 73, 75, 76, 77

T

terra cotta flue liners, 73, 122, 139, 154, 174

throat damper, ix, 51, 53, 68

top damper, see dampers

trees, 159, 193, 198

U

US Consumer Products Safety Commission, 61

The Inside Story, A Guide to Indoor Air Quality, 61

V

velocity of flue gases, 9-10

W

Warren, David J.N., 124, 128

wood, 151–52, 158, 160, 174

hard, 151, 160

soft, 151, 160

varieties of, 160

WS 5/16

CPSIA information can be obtained
at www.ICGtesting.com
Printed in the USA
LVOW12s1913260416

485420LV00001B/87/P